Let us therefore do what alone we
can do: bring light to the earth,
"be the light of the earth"! And
to that end we have our wings and
our speed and severity; for this
are we virile and even terrible
like fire. Let those be terrified
by us who do not know how to gain
light and warmth from us!

Friedrich Nietzsche
The Gay Science

T0336306

Fornalutx

Selected Poems, 1928–1990

IRVING LAYTON

Introduction by Brian Trehearne

McGill-Queen's University Press
Montreal & Kingston • London • Buffalo

© Irving Layton 1992
ISBN 0-7735-0952-6 (cloth)
ISBN 0-7735-0963-1 (paper)

Legal deposit fourth quarter 1992
Bibliothèque nationale du Québec

Printed in Canada on acid-free paper

Publication of this book has been supported
by the Canada Council through its Block
Grant program.

Canadian Cataloguing in Publication Data

Layton, Irving, 1912–
Fornalutx: selected poems, 1928–1990
ISBN 0-7735-0952-6 (bound) –
ISBN 0-7735-0963-1 (pbk.)
I. Title.
PS8523.A95A6 1992   C811'.54   C92-090515-3
PR9199.3.L39A6 1992

Typeset in Aldus 11/14
by Caractéra production graphique inc.,
Quebec City

Contents

Abbreviations

BCOP	*The Bull Calf and Other Poems*, 1956
BH	*The Black Huntsmen*, 1951
BOAJ	*Balls for a One-Armed Juggler*, 1963
BP	*The Blue Propeller*, 1955
Cerb.	*Cerberus*, 1952
CGE	*The Cold Green Element*, 1955
CP	*Collected Poems*, 1965
CPIL	*The Collected Poems of Irving Layton*, 1971
DH	*Droppings from Heaven*, 1979
EOBN	*Europe and Other Bad News*, 1981
FMBJ	*For My Brother Jesus*, 1976
FR	*Final Reckoning: Poems, 1982–1986*, 1987
GB	*The Gucci Bag*, 1980 (limited edition)
GB²	*The Gucci Bag*, 1983 (McClelland and Stewart edition)
HN	*Here and Now*, 1945
IB	*The Improved Binoculars*, 1956
IB²	*The Improved Binoculars* (2d edition), 1956
LCW	*Love the Conqueror Worm*, 1953
LLM	*Lovers and Lesser Men*, 1973

Introduction

FORNALUTX

"Fornalutx," the poem from which this volume takes its title, conveys the clash of joyful expectation and frustrated desire that lies at the heart of this retrospective collection of the poems of Irving Layton. The poem opens with ironic simplicity as if from a casual tourist's diary, describing the foreign villa to which the poet has travelled. From the "oven of light" into which the villa's name translates the poet had expected "paradisal bliss," a place where "the ripe fruit-bearing trees" invite the plucking fingers. Instead he arrives at a place where the sun – beloved Layton image of passionate desire – is "vile" and smokes like an extinguished cinder, exuding a darkness that makes the cheeks "pallid" (an inverse reminder of the "etiolation" by lack of sun that curses the *Massenmenschen* of Layton's other poems). Its heat is "numbing" rather than sensually invigorating, and the faceless wanderers in its glare are "the damned." The vicinity of the house is imaged as hell itself by the speaker, who calls up the *bolge* of Dante's Inferno when he sees "the terraced hills" and inhales the aroma of "excrement" and "rotting matter under [his] feet." The tourist's dreams of "a fabulous realm" are thus abruptly punctured: his descent from the imagined villa to the real one is a Lucifer's plunge from the paradise of desire to the hell of reality. For Layton, it is as significant a damnation as any to be found in "Dante's famous rungs."

This poem's bitter descent, with its rich epic overtones, may be taken as an emblem of Irving Layton's poetic vision and nature. In it are contained his instinctual readiness for joy and its persistent confounding by the sour earth on which he finds himself. Here is his willingness to damn; here too are his favoured symbols, twisted by a vile human nature into sources of suffering and confusion. Here is that striking casualness of tone that disguises the meticulous rhythmic expression of his poems. And here, too, is the self-irony that has generated his most successful and compelling poetry, for this speaker has been (and will always be) damned by the intensity of his desire for the "fabulous realm" of his imagination realized. The traveller's freedom to move between these worlds of "winter" and blinding heat, of anticipation and bitter reality – and his unmitigated bafflement each time they are found dissonant – creates such ironies, involving the poet crucially in his condemnations of others. By no means does Layton offer "Fornalutx" as his own prophetic transcendence of this infernal region. The speaker falls as well, but only after having again revealed the persistent and joyful naïveté with which he envisions the possible pleasures of his lapsarian world. Layton is at once the superior visitor of true knowing and the mistaken traveller whose idealisms are his own worst worldly punishment.

Thus Layton consigns us all to an "oven of light" – a place of burning and of illumination – that he inhabits with us, his consciousness of human cruelty and soullessness the only safeguard that keeps him joyful and creative. Perhaps it is this vision more than any other aspect of his art that has shocked his Canadian readership, who have often enough sought to damn him in return. But such readers must miss the curious humility that marks Layton's voice; not just in the irony of mistakenness that typifies the Layton personae, but in the poet's wry refusal to articulate the summary truths implied by his visions of Fornalutx. This poem ends not with prophetic platitude but with a hanging question: "What truth did Fornalutx wish to say?" The dualisms that energize the poem until its final stanza – of winter and summer, paradise and hell, the poet and the damned – are thus not reconciled in its closure. Although it is made clear that the poet did not come to his hateful villa "by chance," and that he had a truth to discover there, neither he nor we are told what this "truth" is. The poem can only close once he acknowledges a lost level of meaning on which the dualisms of his vision are submitted to a larger purpose, even if that purpose remains intangible. Layton rarely propounds the cosmic truths which so many poets consider it their duty to describe; he is vigorously a poet of this world and its crude mechanisms of pleasure and pain. But he also refuses to accept as his own metaphysics the endless meaningless recurrence of such dualities, recognizing in that later Nietzschean premise the frustration of his own expansive and exuberant ego. Thus he points continually, as he does here, to whispered meanings that evade us in our own temporal vortices of desire and disappointment.

"Fornalutx" stands as an appropriate invitation into this volume of Layton's selected poems. As he is not a poet who attempts to seal off his visions on the metaphysical level, a true selection of his poems will necessarily include a greater variety of voices and themes, often in apparent contradiction, than those of poets whose *oeuvre* works towards the ever more comprehensive and inclusive truths to which a selection may then be pointed. On the scale extending from the imagined "fabulous realm" to the horrific and damnable Fornalutx are infinite points of departure for the Layton poem. All such poems will participate in the "fallen" condition of Fornalutx itself, oscillating between celebration and horror, between the oven and the light. But the volume as a whole, gathering up such antinomies as the life-long envisioning of a single poetic man, projects that unheard truth that Fornalutx whispered with "its foul breath." It emerges as the reader's task to attend to these manifold Laytonic voices and gather them up into the larger projected truth that remains unspoken among their resonances.

The selection of Layton's work within this volume therefore has among its purposes the extension of his canon to include a wider range of such voices. Layton's most familiar and thoroughly received poems are not included here. They have become – for their genius – too securely representative of Layton to too many readers. In a culture in which literary reputation rests almost entirely in the hands of academics, there is a great urge to conformity and continuity – to tradition – in our responses to our poets. "The Birth of Tragedy" and "A Tall Man Executes a Jig" are unquestionably among Layton's greatest poems. But they have been so often anthologized and so frequently interpreted that they may have temporarily lost the ability to shock and to stimulate that was so important to their composer. The less familiar verse included in *Fornalutx* will provide new challenges to Layton's established readership as much as it will reach beyond that readership to new audiences, perhaps prepared at last to hear Layton's less correct and meditative tones.

The Layton of the universities is after all the essentially Nietzschean Layton, the poet whose vision of man's cruelty and self-inflation is mediated by an intellectual affinity with the German philosopher who now – coincidentally – has become seminal to academic literary theory. Layton is among Canada's most sensitive and effective interpreters of Nietzschean ethics and aesthetics, and he was belatedly recognized as a significant new Canadian poet in the late 1950s, after a period in which Nietzsche had inspired some of his most powerful lyrics. But Layton's rage and disgust at humankind's demonic history are not always contained within the appreciable boundaries of German philosophy; his language of vituperation is not always as serenely meditative as the diction of his Nietzschean lyrics. Poems in which the vision of, say, "The Cold Green Element" is expressed in profane language, in less elaborate rhythms, with less obvious formal complexity, have not been heard by Layton's critics and readers. Despite the pared-down immediacy of voice in the poems in this volume, his deliberative control of rhythm and music is as crucial here as it is to the better-known works, but in the latter the stylistic mastery is more obvious and has therefore been more frequently remarked by the critics. The result is a rather distorted "popular" Layton, an essentially philosophical poet whose anger is containable and referable to an established intellectual and poetic tradition. The less popular Layton of "Fornalutx" – that is to say, the poet whose manner and voice are far more various and less decorous than the anthologies persuade us – has been disappearing from critical view of late. This volume should provide those readers who wish a truer and more vital response to the poetry of Irving Layton the passionate, uncontainable and discomfiting poems they crave – the poems that truly represent the full range and popular power of Layton's creativity.

Chief among the little-heard voices that fill this volume is Layton's ongoing rage at the stupidity and evil of human nature. No other Canadian poet has written so many poems of damnation and disgust; indeed, the genre itself (if something so random and idiosyncratic in target and form should be called a genre) is practically unknown in Canada. As in a previous age Layton had to fight to establish himself against the genteel versifiers of the Canadian Authors' Association, so now he must fight for his place within a contemporary poetic tradition that privileges maudlin confessionalism and/or hyper-intellectualized self-reflexivities. In neither "tradition" are civic and spiritual responsibilities the poet's burden. Layton has always identified this lack in our poetry as uniquely Canadian, arising from the persistence of Loyalist and bourgeois influences on our intellectual history, but in fact it is a broader problem, a modern problem of authority and self-consciousness. To criticize his or her age a poet must assume a consolidated and ultimately superior position within it, and that is an egoism that makes poets of our nineties, academically correct to a fault, blanch to the bone. Layton has had no such crisis of self-legitimation.

In general, Layton's *cris de coeur* of social and political outrage appeared in the 1960s and thereafter, once his initial working out of Nietzschean ethics had generated some of his most striking poems. Layton found himself suddenly popular in his own country and read around the world, but at the same time in need of a social and political basis for his philosophy. Poetry that had in the 1950s been largely a celebration of the passionate individual suddenly flowered in the 1960s into a social and global consciousness that took an accounting of the various agents of evil arrayed against such passion. In keeping with the romantic insurrections of that decade, Layton used his cultural authority to denounce now recognizable injustices: the barbarisms of Stalinism, the ready proliferation of military technology and the Arab alliance's failed attacks against Israel in the late sixties. (It is a key to the nature of Layton's social conscience that he now decries Israel just as vehemently for its treatment of the Palestinians within its post-1967 borders.) Throughout the decade, as well, his historical consciousness of the horrors of the Holocaust became increasingly acute and issued in some of his most painful and pain-giving utterances.

Much of this prophetic and condemnatory poetry was misunderstood by the Layton readers who had finally canonized him after the publication of *A Red Carpet for the Sun* in 1958. Prominent critics such as A.J.M. Smith and Northrop Frye had found in the Layton of the fifties a Romantic individualist malleable enough to be brought into line with their favoured preconceptions of the nature and use of poetry (although in Smith's case this required some intellectual acrobatics that Louis Dudek later decried on Layton's behalf). But for neither critic was there room in the language of poetry for the social, political and economic excoriations Layton was launching in volumes like *Periods of the Moon* (1967) and *The Shattered Plinths* (1968). Although this material found an excited new readership even as it surrendered a portion of the old, Layton considered its reception to be of a piece with the prudish reaction by the Canadian literary establishment to his earliest poems of sexual and romantic love. Thus his 1960s forewords launch their diatribes against a generalized Canadian consciousness whose restrictive codes of individual behaviour repressed at one fell swoop the libidinous and the politicized, the confessional and the public poet.

But there was crucial grist for Layton's mill in this rejection of his new voices. It has always been important for Layton's creative drive to conceive himself as outside an established power structure that rejects him. The success, indeed notoriety, of the late 1950s threatened to engulf that premise in an excess of adulation (tinged albeit with a typically Canadian lack of close reading). By expanding the voice of rage in the sixties Layton guaranteed himself a host of nay-sayers whose reactions to his new work – essentially aesthetic and formalist – could be in turn satirized and thus generate new energy for subsequent volumes of poetry. This dialectic of acceptance and rejection (by both poet and audience) lies at the heart of the famous Layton concept of the "murdered selves" that make up his being. The poet is not a contained and fixed being whose attributes, once poetically exposed, are exhausted: he is an eternally regenerating *vates* whose relations with the world produce violence – he is murdered – and rebirth – he is resurrected by decrying murder.

The "raised voice" is not the only Layton to be heard in this collection. Indignation is only one possible poetic response to the horrors of Fornalutx. Another is elegy, and Layton is among the most successful elegiac poets Canada has produced. He mourns the loss of those who are trampled by the brute energy of human historical process, the Jews, slain animals, brutalized artists. In seeking to resurrect their slaughtered voices he sometimes modulates his own anger and relates to his subjects with gentleness, perhaps ironic but always tender. He is also frequently elegiac in middle and later volumes about his own past selves – about the loss of childhood, of innocence, of first love, of firm flesh and bone. In such gentler pieces his philosophical ground is Heraclitean: all matter is aflame and consumes even as it renews itself. From this perspective the given local agents of human decay are insignificant: it is our temporal natures that Layton addresses here, and common mortality fills his voice with sympathy.

But from the same perspective it is possible to celebrate the present day – for the very brevity of its wonders – before it is consumed by the flames or put to torture in the hands of brutes. Those who would seek to "redeem" Layton's poetry from its harsher chords will find here their melody in the joyous sensual responsiveness to life that has always energized his poetry. A more intuitive and whole response to the two voices would recognize, however, that without a passionate adoration of life and the human individual it would be impossible for him to feel outrage when they are destroyed by others who have blinded themselves to compassion. Nor is it possible to celebrate keenly and exuberantly without some recognition that the thing celebrated – a graceful animal, a woman's body, a moment of late sunlight at the tree's height – can be ruined and made hideous in a second by the intervention of dark human purposes. There is no discontinuity, then, no necessary rupture, between the poles of celebration and damnation: they have their common nourishment in Layton's passionate worship of the life force that binds human, animal and vegetable nature in a nexus of spontaneous joy. Redemption from horror, for those who seek it in Layton's vision, lies chiefly in that energy.

These are the voices of the visionary Layton, whose subject is humankind, whose perspective is global and broadly ethical. Their juxtapositions in this volume reveal the intimate interrelationships among them. But there are quieter and more local Layton tones as well, poems which target social and cultural rather than spiritual and psychological conditions. Satire is among the earliest of Layton's manners, tracing its roots to his first publication, *Here and Now* (1945). There a fairly routine youthful leftism underpins a number of satiric portraits of proletarian, immigrant and bourgeois life. But the critical response (or lack of one) to Layton's first dozen volumes gave him an object of satiric attack that was to prove tantalizing for the balance of his career. No other Canadian poet has been so unyieldingly harsh to the academic and literary communities so important to his reputation, or has identified so blatantly the inherent impediments to freedom of thought that (ironically) support an academically sanctioned national literature. From these critical refusers of the feast Layton was able to broaden his castigations to take in all those who, like the initiatory critics, refused the energy of the passionate poet and sought the means of silencing him: the lawyers, poetasters, bourgeoisie and false readers of his half-century career. From anathema to a teasing laughter, Layton's satiric manner exposes in such social clusters the hypocrisy of motive and action to which the poet himself – independent of their general motive, which is profit – is not subject.

In all of these manners the Layton persona is key to expression and interpretation of the poem. The speaking voice harangues and is aggressive in its passions and denunciations, dinning itself powerfully into our ears so that we are forced into enlightenment or angry dismissal of his vision. But a selected Layton would not be complete – would misrepresent the poet the volume must candidly represent – if it did not include a selection of the impersonal Layton, the poet whose self-effacement from his own poems can be astonishingly gentle. Although Layton never adopted imagist doctrines wholeheartedly, it is possible to see in the poems that open this volume (and, less obviously, but certainly, in those that follow) a delicacy of observation and humility of self-representation that popular reputation does not routinely associate with Layton. Such poems need our contemplation, clearly, when we form our responses to his work. It is too easy to associate the "raised voice" with the representative Layton tone and to lose touch with the refinements of emotion and perception that fill the individual images of his longer poems. There is a startling gentleness of detail and fineness of style even in the poems of outrage that we are perhaps best made to recognize by seeing it first in isolation, when the Layton persona has removed himself from the poem's margins and the phenomenal world stands transfigured by his absent eye.

These selected poems demonstrate, then, the breadth, diversity and mastery of Layton's poetry. It should prove impossible for his careful readers to select one or the other of these voices as the "true" Laytonic tone. His vitality of poetic experimentation allows him to fly the nets we raise against him. The dissonance and interpenetration of his many voices will lead us close, if we respond well, to that "truth" that Fornalutx whispered in his ear, but no single poem or cluster of poems will pronounce the last word on his poetry. Like him, we are trapped in the eternal dualism of imaginative desire and bitter reality as we turn his pages; but we are offered the reassurance of his magnanimity, compassion and joyousness that there is a reason for passing through this "oven of light" – that we too will come to admit the unheard truth that resonates in the life-long passions of a profoundly moral man.

VISION

The unity of Layton's variety lies, then, in his reverence for the individual in a condition of joyful liberty. When that joy is preserved, Layton is its celebrant; when it is trampled, he is its outraged defender and chief mourner. Within these parameters he has worked out an entirely idiosyncratic ethics, the delineation of which is an important task for his present and future readers. It is dissonant with the Layton reputation that I speak of him as an ethical thinker, of course, and I do so deliberately in order to suggest the principles of value that underpin the whole of the present volume. Layton is not, of course, a moralist, one whose chief concern is the quotidian behaviour of the human subject in his social relations; his ethical inquiries are larger, of good and evil and their sources and manipulation in that social sphere. He will not accept the conventional polarities of moral behaviour and superficial guilt-systems; these are no more than

> An obsession with a nice scent
> unknown among nature's great laws:
> yet what men call good and evil
> is but nail polish on their claws

("Nail Polish")

But even as he corrects such hypocrisies he implies an alternate vision of good and evil that his readers should elaborate. It is on this basis that he has often characterized his poetry as prophetic in nature, rejecting as it does the conventional morality of his corrupt day in order to enunciate a higher, harsher wisdom.

Evil in Layton's vision is Satanic only in its infernal applications to the infinitely rackable body and soul. In the world of

xxiv

"Fornalutx" there is no cosmic principle of evil to which cruelty and nihilism must be referred for an explanation; evil is of this earth, and we are its agents. It has its roots for the most part in stupidity and ignorance and frustration, out of which it is human "nature" to strike in resentment at innocent others:

> The senseless ones are never by design
>   evil; but get in your way
> like the ugly stumps of trees; order
>   bad taste or out of boredom
> start long wars [...]
>
> ("The Way of the World")

A more profound evil is conceivable, however, for there are those who, like Hitler – "the most ferocious beast / in creation" ("Mount Royal Cemetery") – are indeed evil by design, and on a scale so colossal that conventional ethics, our idealism and our cynicisms, are entirely eradicated:

> After Auschwitz and Gulag
> who can be cynical? [...]
>
> Nowadays we know
> perversities of every kind
> horrendous brutality
> lies treacheries betrayals
> the delights of sadistic impotence
> are normal [...]
>
> ("Runts")

But should the monstrosity of a Hitler be the root henceforth of all ethical inquiry? Did that bestial nature loom so large over all humankind that a Satanic cosmic principle was unleashed after all? Layton denies the premise, and responds by locating the source of Hitler's epic evil in a mind and soul so pitifully minute that he is superhuman by inversion only, by the intense smallness of his humanity:

> Runts are the problem,
> runts who long for the stride and stature

of giants; who hate all truth-telling mirrors.
History demonstrates
outbreaks of runtishness
occur with rhythmic periodicity [...]

Without denying its extreme expression in Nazism, this inter-
pretation keeps evil within the human context; not even a Hitler
testifies to a cosmic force that operates on passive and innocent
humankind. To seek such a force – to call it Satan and posit its
opponent God – is to seek "nail polish" for the human "claws"
that are the true source of cruelty in the world.

Such readings of evil offer limited comfort, of course, and
Layton is the first to acknowledge and express his bafflement at
the range and technology of human cruelty. So much of that
cruelty is thoughtless; so much is perpetrated by apparently
civilized men with loved families and words of culture and
decency ready to their lips:

As if he had done this
many times before,
the stranger dislodged the flat stone
near his hand
and let it crash down heavily
on the hopping bird [...]

"That makes an exciting composition,"
observed the stranger.

("Still Life")

Perhaps it was the bird's "joyfully ignoring" both poet and
stranger that led to this indifferent act of violence; Layton's
obvious identification with the bird's joy renders him equally
vulnerable to the faceless stranger's stones. Similar incongruities
of cultivation and cruelty are depicted in Layton's portrait of a
group of Nazi officers' execution of Jewish children:

Smiles, affectionate pats
soften the chilfren's faces;
gifts of dolls, toy trains [...]

> When the last glimmer of suspicion
> fades, the officers whip out
> their revolvers
> and start shooting.
>
> ("Aesthetic Cruelty")

This is the conjunction that most astonishes Layton, of sensitivity to aesthetic form and brutality to life itself. Can such a contradiction of nature be explained only as a frustration of will?

If the refined individual and his capacity for random evil cannot finally be rationalized, the poet may leap to a more collective denunciation in which all of humankind is arraigned in a prophetic vision of apocalyptic consequence:

> There are still regions on our planet
> human blood has not made wet
> valleys and mountains that have not heard
> the sound of human groans and wailings
> forests that have never witnessed
> human treachery and human vindictiveness
> sunsmitten gorges that have not echoed and re-echoed
> with the searing cries of hate and triumphant carnage
>
> ("The Coming of the Messiah")

The ironic point of the title is of course that the Messiah will only come to earth when every inch of ground under our feet is red with the blood we have ourselves spilled: a point of last judgment which will already have taken us beyond any Messiah's redemption.

Whatever the sources and consequences of human evil, Layton's constant purpose is to bring it before our eyes. Perhaps nothing terrifies him more than the human ability, *via* religion, political ideology or desensitizing media, to deflect the horror that evil should cause in us. He counters with poems that force us back to those horrors we deny so skilfully:

> You must say to yourself
> this is not film, this is real

and it's happening to a man
who was once an infant and cried in the dark

Those are real intestines
spilling out into his hand;
the pain and terror are real

("The Lesson")

If he has written poem after poem of Holocaust horror or has reiterated the cruelty of humankind to animals in so many lines it is because his cultivated and aesthetic audience displays such astounding detachment from the violence of his world. Poetry has become, he fears, a vehicle of that detachment, an intellectualized region into which a few dozen Canadians wander in order to be protected from the horrors of truth-telling. But Layton's readers will receive no such comfort:

For I do not write to improve your soul;
    or to make you feel better, or more humane;
Nor do I write to give you new emotions;
Or to make you proud to be able to experience them
    or to recognize them in others.
I leave that to the fraternity of lying poets [...]

("Whom I Write For")

Other poets will make their verses out of private emotions or intellectual and aesthetic inquiries: Layton's are

made
from charred bones,
the smiles of fair-haired
humans
looking at them

("The Lyric")

The ironic versification of "The Lyric" reveals what an ambivalent word "human" has become in Layton's lexicon, divorced as it is so often from the "humanity" it ought to signify.

Layton's most poignant representations of the victims of human cruelty are not of other humans but of the various animals, tortured, starved, clubbed and eaten, that humans wreak their misguided frustrations upon. These are among his most famous images, of course, perhaps epitomized in the "violated grass snake" in "A Tall Man Executes a Jig." The bird stoned by a visiting stranger above is only one such example; the "Molibos Cat" and its catalogued suffering shows once again the inanity and pointlessness of human cruelty:

> Dogs don't suddenly kick a pregnant cat
> for no reason at all
> or blind her with a pointed stick.
> No dog ever poured naphthalene on her fur
> and afterwards put a lighted match to her tail.
> No dog ever wanted to hobble her for life
> by sawing off one of her front paws.
>
> She has been around humans for a long time
> and knows their true nature [...]
>
> ("Molibos Cat")

The cruelty of nature "red in tooth and claw" – the traditional war of dog and cat – is here revealed to bear no comparison with the bloody-mindedness of human beings looking to fill a quiet afternoon. Curiously, it is in his relation with these innocent animals that Layton is most willing to incriminate himself, along with his fellows, for inexplicable cruelty: in "Therapy" the speaker's bludgeoning of a happy young badger "rummaging in our garbage bin / for food" earns him the poet's corrosive closing irony when he concludes that he is "now strong enough for God and Man." He is indeed strong enough for a man: strong enough to kill without reason a weaker, joyful creature. In "Encounter" the poet's initial feeling of protectiveness towards a lizard, "an embossed aristocratic device" clinging to the wall, is shown to have its roots in his own meaningless desire to wreak violence upon the animal:

> Is it because
> I really wish to kill him,
> to pierce with a nail
> and mess up his trim armorial? [...]

Go away, lizard, go away.
There are tears in my eyes.
It is dangerous for you to stay.

A typical Layton irony reveals that tears in a man's eyes are no protection for those he might choose to destroy.

Another helpless victim of human nature is the poet himself, and as Layton has experienced that treatment at first hand he is all too aware of the urge to destroy the creative principle that lurks in the hearts of humans. Artists are killed as pointlessly as animals; they offer as little real threat to those who have authority over them. The fate of Italian film director Pier Paolo Pasolini draws the parallel starkly, his animal body literally crushed:

Your beautiful Marxist head
                         smashed
lies in the dark wood

The chilled red cells
that once held the passion of Christ,
a dream of social justice
                         indiscriminately wet
dirt road, insensate twigs and grass
the lout's crude wooden bat

("The Violent Life")

Pasolini is the whole martyr; for other artists a perhaps worse because less complete torture remains:

Everyone laughed when he told the assembly
how the famous rebel poet was captured.

[...] they had pulled his ears
away from the skull
and made him chew and swallow them,
first one and then the other.

("Moutarde")

The hellish symbolism of a torture which removes the poet's ability to hear the indecencies of his captors reveals that Layton's is a war of expansive metaphor against materialist literalism. Those who seek a total system to which life may be submitted for resolution and clarity must destroy those who recognize life's fluidity of meaningfulness and celebrate it in the multeity of poetry.

Animals and artists thus stand in Layton's ethics for those whose creative vitality is sacrificed at the hands of ignorant, joyless and frustrated "runts" seeking to prove their grandeur. The only evil he will acknowledge and loosely define is the evil that seeks to stifle joy in all its forms; the only good he will live by is that very joy, despite its vulnerability in the social and "human" world. These ideas have their roots in Layton's Nietzscheanism, of course, with its identification of "Socratism," that is, rationalist linearity and logical analysis, and "Christianity," the misinterpreted teachings of Jesus, as chief among the forces of limitation and repression, and with its division of human nature into the few *Übermenschen* and the many *Massenmenschen* who align themselves respectively with the "joyful wisdom" of the animals and artists or with the passive brutality of its suppressors. Like Nietzsche, Layton is not concerned to particularize the routines of good and evil, for in a sense his ethics also move beyond such polarities. In any given moment in the historical continuum the exuberant joy by which he is defined may be called evil or good by his contemporaries and applauded or punished. But he also – again like Nietzsche – refuses utter nihilism, for as a particular artist at a particular historical moment he is determined and his decisions enforced by patterns of intellectual, moral and cultural training which he cannot escape. Thus Layton will rail, vituperate and denounce the local evils he witnesses, even if in the purist form of his ethics he must acknowledge the cyclical and dialectical nature of the battle between joy and destruction.

For despite their recognition of those dialectics Layton and other *Übermenschen* are spared nothing – neither death nor decay. In adherence to these ethics there is no eventual paradise or worldly state of grace and election. In a volume of poems selected as late in a poet's life as this – Layton will reach eighty before the volume appears – the gradual descent into age and the imminence of his own death are notes that sound more intensely than ever. In the cycle of "murdered selves" he has already died and been reborn many times, and even in old age that process continues: a backyard "glimpse" of his beautiful neighbour's "white panties," for instance, shows the inevitability of regeneration as long as the flesh persists:

What does it mean?
Plainly, my dearest friends,
that once again
    I must begin
all over again

("The Glimpse")

This is the Layton miracle at its best, the endless preparedness for joy and its regeneration that he will take to the grave. But "The Glimpse" is also the self-elegy of a man who has lived the senses passionately and now knows their keenness to be waning, and he laments that loss as passionately as he celebrates his moments of persistent pleasure. A visit to Paros in the Aegean in 1985 reveals the intimate connection between the two kinds of responsiveness:

You bend to remove the beachpebble
from your sandal;
and as you straighten to greet me,
your smile, showing your strong white teeth,
reminds me I trod these shores once before [...]

The same barren hills and widening sea;
the same rumpled many-color'd Joseph's coat,
the same, yet not the same.

For now, my face a warrior's Achaean mask,
it is I who invest these hills, this sea,
with their boundless calm.

("The Investiture")

In the age that has been stamped on his face – still the face of a "warrior" – he finds a new calm; not the elderly meditative detachment of Socrates, who was "glad to be freed from the vicious taskmaster" of his sexuality, but the calm earned by a life-long dedication to his sexual nature. His aged voice is never tinged with regret for what might have been. This is the elder poet who cries, "Spry and drugged with love / I pole-vault / over my grave."

Death after all may be fair cause for celebration when Layton considers that all humankind – torturers and butchers as well as artists – will come to the same end:

> I know your way
> with oligarchs and despots; you
> let them posture a short while
> and then you say 'Come' and quietly they go
>
> ("When Death Says 'Come'")

The peace and rest of death may also be attractive to a poet who has spent his whole life sensitive to the cycles of joy and suffering perpetuated in the human story:

> Tombs, I say, are reassuring when men
> are swine, smiling wolves with capped teeth,
> the cities reeking of scribbling whores
> and those who need no bribes to pimp for them.
>
> ("Final Reckoning: After Theognis")

For many of those trampled under the jackboots of history the grave and tomb are places themselves of a quiet sensual beauty:

> Yet these blank eyes sculpted
> from grove and hill and rock
> before which the centuries have passed unseen
> comfort me; inuring me, I say,
> to the sorrows our humanity
> compels us to inflict on each other.
> They teach me to live the free hours with gusto.
>
> ("Etruscan Tombs")

There is the connection back to Layton's sensual and celebratory nature. Paradoxically, the harmony and beauty of death's images teach us to revel passionately and without caution in life's sensual offerings. Only by living with "gusto" will we come to the tomb ready for its restfulness; those who approach it without having lived passionately will not welcome that stillness and peace.

The mortality that unites all humanity also motivates the paradoxes of cruelty and joyfulness that Layton portrays. The destructive agents of totalitarian repressiveness fight their awareness of death by building systems of power that contain all that can be controlled by human energy. The agents of joy and creativity, if anything more aware of their ends, respond to this life with deep pleasure precisely because it is finite and its sudden violent closure is always potential in their actions. This paradox gives rise to Layton's ironic view of humankind as

> Soul encased in rotting flesh
> god with an asshole
> he shapes the humbling stool
> into catafalque and bomb,
> immortal poem

("The Absurd Animal")

In the three final images of "The Absurd Animal" are the points of the triangle I have implied: the catafalque on which the dead are displayed, the bomb flung by those joy-destroyers who cannot accept their mortality, and the "immortal poem" written in the life of the *Übermensch* or literally posed on the page.

The faces of violence and evil are, as Layton has shown us, infinite in their variety and complex in their cruelty. The faces of joy are perhaps fewer and certainly subtler in their manifestations. In the Layton *oeuvre* the chief sources of joy are sexual and natural; beauty in its variety (especially the beauty of women, now and then the beauty of men as in "Ganymede," but just as often the beauty of the natural world in conjunction with the attuned poet's senses) and our seizing that beauty for our own regeneration are the meaningful grounds of our existence. These are to be celebrated again and again as each successive self returns to the world after its murder and renewal.

But the artist has a unique and extraordinary role in this process, for he or she not only responds to but also creates beauty for the pleasure of others. In this model of gift-taking and self-giving Layton finds his most eloquent vision of the artist's place in the inescapable cycles of meaningless human energy: there is a sacrifice of selfhood involved which nevertheless makes of the artist the emblem of humankind:

> Drawing a roseleaf for ten years
> I flowed at last into the leaf;
> I shuddered at the raindrop's touch
> till I became raindrop and splash:
> now I draw the roseleaf perfectly

> ("Ch'an Artist")

From this moment of aesthetic exchange between beautiful roseleaf and self-submissive artist emerges a moment of perfection possible through no other human agency.

This contemplative draftsman need not be taken, however, for Layton's essential artist; in keeping with his persistent multiplicity of understanding he recognizes that artists will exist in innumerable relations to the world in which they live. "Modern Greek Poet" and "Herzl," for instance, show that there is no necessary disjunction between artistic genius and political action, and Layton has certainly found that kind of activism attractive when compared with the esoteric and cloistered nepotisms of his Canadian contemporaries. Perhaps he takes it too quickly for granted that a fine artist will make a more noble than average political leader, but his emphasis remains on the artistry that justifies the actions taken: Layton does not seek to emulate the Greek poet but instead after hearing of his practical actions asks to see "everything he had written." Poetry remains the final point.

Layton would reject, however, any apotheosis that tended to grant the artist a superiority to be counted on. He maintains the artist's necessary humility in the face of world indifference by treating himself with a persistent irony that shows the limits of *any* human understanding of universal purposes. He does not hear the whispered truth of Fornalutx; instead he is swamped with its "foul breath." He is a man caught in a time and place which make their own strenuous demands on his sensitive nature, and he is as often caught up in petty squabbles with his critics and relatives as any other citizen. He is not himself a Herzl, nor a Jew of the camps: he is instead an urban Canadian, well-worked and well-travelled to be sure, whose immediate world is not one of atrocity but of irritation. In the *personae* he has adopted both in poetry and in public to deal with that irritation he has necessarily seen himself ironically, as must all *Übermenschen* forced to temporize with the mass culture of their times.

But he has produced even from the smallest of disagreements the material of a great body of poetry, and in that consciousness he finds the pole-vault that will help him in his final leap over the grave. He may be surrounded by misunderstanding and folly and invective, but he will respond with a volume of poems like this, launch a conflagration with his times, knowing and teaching that

> Out of rubbish burning and burning comes
> Mozartian ecstasy leaping with the flames.
>
> ("Esthetique")

Few poets of this or any time or country have pursued their ecstasies so whole-heartedly as Layton. His Canadian readers have not always been pleased with that burden of his song; they have been trained to receive a more definitive and more moderate philosophy in their poets. Layton will not respond. He is perhaps akin to the butterfly of "Nominalist," "sailing evenly between / warring schools of philosophy." And he is the butterfly's visionary as well, lifting his eyes in a final desire to

> [...] the remote sky
> from which no conclusions
> may ever be drawn.

The play on "conclusion" here aptly completes the Layton cycle: for only the poet who refuses conclusions can himself welcome the conclusion of a long life. It is not an easy nor ever a clear philosophy, but its rarity suggests how vital Layton is to the world's contemporary poetry.

Brian Trehearne
McGill University

Fornalutx

We came, sent by friends we respected.
The house, of course, was decent enough;
But heat and flies were unexpected,
Nor was water seen for cooling off.

The terraced hills made one think of hell:
I have in mind Dante's famous rungs;
Excrement, not brimstone, was the smell
When the foul air entered in our lungs.

And all winter we had planned for this;
In thought had made of it a place
Where running in paradisal bliss
We plucked the ripe fruit-bearing trees.

Who thought of the heat-stained cobblestone?
The damned who shuffled on the street?
And cheeks made pallid by a vile sun,
And rotting matter under one's feet?

We dreamed, yes, we dreamed of Fornalutx,
A fabulous realm, Oven of Light:
And indeed from shard and glass came shoots
Of numbing heat, so the name was right.

Or but half so, for the very dust
From plastered walls and the well-worn steps
Seemed buried in a film of green rust.
Light? O no! More like dark perhaps.

But that too is not quite accurate:
I mean about the dark. The sun smoked.
That's the nearest I can come to it.
And no air stirred, and we almost choked.

Yet was it by chance that we came there,
And crossed oceans for a misspent day?
Or putting its foul breath to my ear.
What truth did Fornalutx wish to say?

THE HALO

The reflection in the still water
of the pines lining the bay's shore
makes a darkgreen ellipsis with them,
a mysterious shimmering hollow

And I am seized by a desire
to strip at once to the cold skin
and swimming into it come out
at the far end of that tree'd halo

But instead I watch from the distance,
standing at the opposite shore,
and see it darken and disappear
and then widen to enfold the stars

Evening ... the feathery grass ... boughs
That coldly lift a silent offering;
The shadowy swaying of trees
Like graceful nuns in a forbidden dance;
The yearning stillness of an ended night.
And clouds the colour of oyster shells
Clustered about a comfortless moon.

Dawn. A crayon held in a master's fingers
Pencilling in soft outlines the earth.
The hills. Humps that tell laconically
The labouring age of earth;
And suns that turn the wayside streams
To moving panes of light.

The fog spreads her grey belly
over the yellow tramcars,
brushes past, on silent feet,
shabby Paint and Hardware stores,
or flattens her wan face
against the illuminated shop window
of department stores.

The fog throws a comradely arm
over a mutilated hydrant
in a deserted square,
in a slum district.

The fog lays her soiled bandages
over the foreheads of failures –
they start as they recognize for the first time
how pitiful they are.

The fog tickles herself
under the armpits
and laughs
inaudibly;
She has
chlorotic gums.

The way his boy plucks them
off the Old Man's net
you'd think they were maybe scales
flakes of mica
or sequins
on a washed-up tulle dress

They're fish
– the tiniest I ever saw
And have just about stopped
squirming
              but for the obstinate few
still hanging on

Tell me
who's the Xenophon
of this Anabasis

Thalassa ... Thalassa ...

They lift and flutter
like coloured bits of paper,
some all the way back to the sea
– if the wind falls that way

For the long-beaked birds
shaped astonishingly
like miniature flying coffins

NOMINALIST

What can I know?

Only this mob of leaves
moving with the breeze,
each fragrant puff of air.

Men's despair and malice
covering the earth
like spears of grass.

Or the traffic's roar
beyond my garden
smelling of fresh rain.

The tremulous black-coated squirrel
all instinct and fear,
unique as the tree's bark.

Or that white butterfly
sailing evenly between
warring schools of philosophy.

Or my own storm-tossed soul,
a troubling joy
since the day I was born.

Finally: the remote sky
from which no conclusions
may ever be drawn.

REDEMPTION

I murdered a bird
of rarer plumage
and delight
than the albatross.

Echoing
in the cold chambers
of the sky,
its final scream
has stunned my ear-drums
for ever.

Forgive, forgive me, woman.

Redemption comes,
but never
in the form
we think it will.

And we are broken
on no wheel
of our own choosing.

STILLNESS

A black pocket comb
and a small bird
lying side by side
off the road

Both covered by a fine dust
and looking unwanted,
the comb no less useless
than the dead bird

Dropped out of someone's pocket
fallen out of the air,
their beauty is the stillness they make
lying in the road dust there

Had it been a drowned child
it should have owned some proof
of birth, and sagacious forbears
    for this neutral water;
      someone to mourn, a name.

But being a rotting fish
its fins, a red streak in the crumpled
water, mattered to no one
    nor the white
      of its decomposing beauty.

Ludicrous its solemnity
on the throbbing water.

PIGEONS

When it begins to drizzle
the pigeons fly to the boughs of trees
where they sit quietly,
pretending they are birds of doom:
wet crows in a charcoal illustration
for a Gothic fable.
Purest illusion!
for with the first beams of light
from a repentant sun
they shake wetness and theatricality
from their tails
to alight once more on grass or gravel
in a fussy search for food; pigeons
are always hungry;
or is it insatiable greed
makes them ceaselessly prod the earth
with their pointed beaks,
their ridiculous slender heads
sawing the world
into two equal and severe halves,
one for each suspicious miser's eye
to take notice of
and disapprove

There is of course
personality.

Animals have it too.

If you stare
long enough
at a flock of goats
you will notice differences.

Or at cows:
one cow's more bovine
than another;
another swings her tail
with nuances of inflection.

At sheep, yes, at sheep
and the lambs
Jesus was gentle with.

And there is also the mouth,
and the large intestine.

THE BLACK TOM

Someone had dragged the dead cat
off the road
and she lay in the rough grass
as though she had fallen asleep in it.
I saw no wheelmarks on her,
no blood on her white and black fur.

The next morning when I came by
she was still lying
curled up in the grass, her head
buried in her forepaws
and looking as if nothing
could ever wake her from her deep slumber.

And today two weeks and thousands
of cars later
the cat's still resting peacefully
on her side,
but now there's some grass between her paws
and the black tom has made her pregnant.

Seeing him pressed against the wall
– an embossed aristocratic device –
why nevertheless
do I feel protective towards him
and his vulnerability
make me want to cry?

Is it because
I really wish to kill him,
to pierce him with a nail
and mess up his trim armorial?
Is that the reason why?
Is that it?

Go away, lizard, go away.
There are tears in my eyes.
It is dangerous for you to stay.

A doctor for mere lucre
performed an unnecessary operation
making my nose nearly
as crooked as himself

Another for a similar reason
almost blinded me

A poet famous
for his lyrics of love
and renunciation
toils at the seduction of my wife

And the humans who would like to kill me
are legion

Only once have I been bitten by a dog.

When I was six
our cat littered behind the stove:
four kittens sound in mind and limb
and one lame.

The lame one
had all my love
– dragging its sick leg
in chase with the others,
all my agonized attention.

It was its playfulness
with a ball
broke my heart at last;
and I was glad
to see the kitten lying, one afternoon,
deadstill
when I returned from school.

Yesterday
for the first time in my life
I axed a young badger
rummaging in our garbage bin
for food.

And though he wobbled
a short distance
before he keeled over,
I am now strong enough for God and Man.

As moles construct
their burrows
and birds their nests,
the lyric poet
invents his own world

With sunsets and petunias
skylarks
a heart a great love
has cracked

Mine's made
from charred bones,
the smiles of fair-haired
humans
looking at them

We were speaking of modern art.

"The human's no longer interesting,"
said the stranger.
"God, nature, man,
we've exhausted them each in turn."

It was a warm August afternoon,
and the linnet kept wiping its beak
on the fallen leaves and grass,
joyfully ignoring both of us.

As if he had done this
many times before,
the stranger dislodged the flat stone
near his hand
and let it crash down heavily
on the hopping bird.

Only the fluttering wing was visible,
and it looked
as if the ridiculous stone
was attempting to fly.

Then stillness: stone on wing: both partly
in shadow.
There was a sweet smell of earth.

"That makes an exciting composition,"
observed the stranger.

Her eyes are round with suspicion.
At your approach she runs away.
Children and grown-ups are her enemy,
not dogs which she can lick in a fair fight

Dogs don't suddenly kick a pregnant cat
for no reason at all
or blind her with a pointed stick.
No dog ever poured naphthalene on her fur
and afterwards put a lighted match to her tail.
No dog ever wanted to hobble her for life
by sawing off one of her front paws.

She has been around humans for a long time
and knows their true nature
– knows it better than Blaise Pascal
who flopped down on his knees and prayed.
Look at her curled up on the ledge;
even in her sleep her long face is reserved and melancholy.

One can imagine Heraclitos, the weeping philosopher,
looking like that.

Like Sieur Montaigne's distinction
between virtue and innocence
what gets you is their unbewilderment

They come into the picture suddenly
like unfinished houses, gapes and planed wood,
dominating a landscape

And you see at a glance
among sportsmen they are the metaphysicians,
intent, untalkative, pursuing Unity

(What finally gets you is their chastity)

And that no theory of pessimism is complete
which altogether ignores them

I knew him for a cultivated
gentleman,
a lover of operas
and a Latinist
who had annotated the De Amicitia
to the acclaim of scholars.

We were in Parc Lafontaine,
admiring the instinctual swans.
There was nothing in his behaviour
– in his walk or talk –
to make me suspicious.

As we passed
the blind woman sitting alone
on one of the benches,
he stopped suddenly before her
and plunged two pins,
one into each cheek.

I heard the blind woman's
terrified shrieks
as he said quietly:
"I can't understand her rage;
my ancestors would have pierced her
with javelins.
She ought to be grateful
we live in a reasonable age."

Of course they put him into the loony bin
where he shares a cell
with a distinguished anthropologist
and one other Latinist.

NAIL POLISH

Seeking for the murderous self
a concealing and sweet perfume,
one will rush to a synagogue,
another dissect a small poem

Or loving himself, a good man
in jest will split a stranger's thighs
then give back with tender moist look
the grin on his mouth as he dies

And some will strike for a frail cause,
proudly burn or unfurl a flag;
amuse dying soldiers in wards,
make love to a love-diseased hag

Who can for truth or justice kill
are the earth's enamoured movers
and they who babble of sweet love
over the bones of their lovers

An obsession with a nice scent
unknown among nature's great laws:
yet what men Call good and evil
is but nail polish on their claws

BEATITUDE

All I require
for my happiness
is a pen
and a sheet of paper
to put down
my unhappy reflections
on men
and the human condition

O queen of the Underworld
with whom poets remain
the better part of the year, hiving insights
in the luminous dark you make for them:
suffer me, a feeble creature
made gracious in your divinity,
to compose a honeycomb
distilled from the tresses of murdered Jewesses,
the sour pollen of human ash.

And may it possess, O dread Immortal,
the fatal taste of truth
whose sharp deceiving sweetness
none may refuse,
enticing the undismayed and forgetful
– the maimed helpers of death –
to a raging death from self-horror.

After the final attack
no one survived
not even the attackers

Over the whole blasted earth
no one was left
to delight in the misery of others

No one but the couple from Ohio:
deaf to her terrified cries
he planted the knife
in his wife's swollen belly

I want nothing
to ever come
between me and the sun

If I see a jetplane
I shall shoot it down

Philosophies
religions:
so many fearful excuses
for not letting the sun
nourish one
and burn him to a cinder

Look at the skeletons
of those oaks:
the proud flame of life
passed through them
without their once having heard
of Jesus or Marx

My son, said the repellant old man,
make certain you never need do
the dirty work of civilization.

All political credos, all religions
are necessary persuasions
to get the poor beggars into the mines.

That a few be whole, many must be broken.
All reform rests on hypocrisy:
fringe benefits for slaves and menials.

Fixed and eternal is the law of gravity:
so, my son, are injustice and the class war.
Living in an affair for aristocrats.

OIL SLICK ON THE RIVIERA
For Milton Wilson

Cowboy in black shirt, black hat, black tie
it rides the waves bucking like a bronco
and will not be thrown.

Let them arch their backs and go suddenly limp;
let their white manes toss wildly,
the froth fall from their mouths; though their fury
is unspent and never-diminishing
it is useless. Nothing
will ever unseat this superb, imperturbable rider.

Or from here is it chimney smoke I see
wind and wave have deflected?
A wavering net strung out along the margin
of the bay
to catch bits of paper and wood, weeds and ferns?
Or is it a funereal graph
for the drownings of vessels and people at sea?

Ah, but the green waves are stubborn, unyielding;
yet no less is the oil slick:
cool as a commissar, dark and crafty as the Georgian
it bides its time, knowing that history will always pardon
whoever has the patience and will-power to only hang on.

MODERN GREEK POET

For A. Vavrikos

In the Aegean night
we drank cold wine
and sat where we could see
the white Acropolis
shedding its useless radiance
like the shattered plinths of a star

And I wasn't the least bit eager
to see any of his poems
until he told me
how in the last civil war
he had single-handedly
killed twelve guerrillas:
the fallen apostles he called them

Then I begged him
to show me
everything he had written

It has taken me long, Lygdamus,
    to learn that humans, barring
a few saints, are degenerate
    or senseless.

The senseless ones are never by design
    evil; but get in your way
like the ugly stumps of trees; order
    bad taste or out of boredom
start long wars
                        where one's counted on
to dredge up manliness, fortitude, and valour
    for their stupefactions.

But wicked are the clever ones.
    Cultured and adept
they will seduce a friend's dear one
with praises of her husband on their lips.

As for the wife
    a little alcohol parts her thighs.
Do not blame her: her husband's name
on the seducer's lips
    makes her the eagerer to satisfy,
teaches her she lies with her very spouse.
And that way is best: no pricks of inwit,
    but the novelty's stab of pleasure is there.

Therefore give me only lovers.
    Come, my latest one, sloe-eyed,
your firm breasts whirling like astonished globes
    before my eyes cross-eyed with lust;
though my legs are bandy
                  the heart's stout
and this provocative member smooth and unwrinkled.
Till the morning parts us, I'll lie beside you
    your nipple at my tired mouth
and one hand of mine
                on your black curling fleece.

Handel composed the MESSIAH
and loved the whores.
Bach was sent to jail for bribery.
Jean Baptiste Lully, thief and swindler,
scored masses and Te Deums
as well as with the princesses of the court.
Corelli was a glutton;
Liszt, a vain seducer.
Carlo Gesualdo who strangled his son,
poisoned his father
and killed his wife
wrote exquisite madrigals
all his life.

When I read somewhere
that Amerigo Vespucci
had been a pork butcher
and finance agent
    in prosperous Florence,
I saw at once
the Muse of History
was a meticulous poet
with a fine sense
of the fitness of things.

It was during
       one of the recurrent famines
brought on by Europe's
       distinguished statesmen & clerics
that the butcher of Konigberg
       sold canned meat
at prices which made the townsfolk
       grab the tins out of his hand.
And it was weeks before they learned
       that they were eating their own children
(ground up Ityluses so to speak)
       that had mysteriously
disappeared from their homes
       never to return;
though a terrible rumour afterwards arose
       in the rest of the country
that the ravenous townspeople had known
       all along and gone on eating
so long as the hacking and packing
       were done by somebody else.

His maintenance is human blood;
mine, luckily, is eel and lamb's kidney,
the succulent livers of young chickens.
Nevertheless, his bigoted taste in food
points me to my appointed place
in Nature's vampyric banquet
whose holiness and justice only
my morbid sentience spoils and poisons.

If your mind isn't stuffed with hamburger
and dills, his crimsoned incisors
and thick blackness make clear
before he turns bat or escaping wolf
how under dying suns life and death
are both equally a pain in the neck,
a wound from which there's no recovery:
we must kill one another and die.

This century's agnostic Faust,
he parleys neither with Devil nor God:
nothing comforts him for love's transiency
or beauty's, their ordered come and go. O
his captivated soul yearns for immortality
and defying Everyman's sentence of doom,
heroically he opens his sooty wings
above green mud, the incredible haunting snow.

They blanket the square like lava
whose seethe only time will still,
or like fallen leaves a wind agitates
on the floor of a forest
before the snows come to tamp them down

In their rage and furor
the kinetic energy of hate, the intoxication
of a million like-minded ciphers
shouting in unison; the camera catches
the eyes glazed by self-righteousness,
the life-enhancing certainty of pillage and murder

It lifts the spirit to know
a hundred years from now
they'll all be dead
and Venus still shine bright and solitary
in the pale evening sky

Corpses fingering blood-stained triggers
seem to the poet a grim charade
who sees the silent, bloated figures
lying like balloons in a parade.

Crushed tanks: their oil bleeding into sand
that a wild molecular frenzy
into dark hieroglyphs changes; and
outlines of a desolate beauty.

Arms raised to salute the victory
by sightless soldiers that have no breath.
Let the victors rejoice; he only
tells them of the cardboard smell of death

I have seen the sombre
alluring eyes
of the caged tigress

Art and love
coral
out of blindest cruelty

And empires
become memorials and cenotaphs,
the subtle smile of history

I have seen a cossack
walk thoughtfully
beside his lamed horse

The sun sinking
bloodied and gorgeous
into the ocean

And summer's violence
stilled in the fruit
my hand reached out to take

One day
I shall tell God
and watch him jump

THE LESSON

This is a finger
This is an eye

Even a small cut causes pain, afterwards soreness;
the terror comes when a bone-shattering bullet
enters the neck, the groin
or the blood rushes after the retreating knife

The thought of death,
of being suddenly reduced to nothing
makes the lips go white

You must say to yourself
this is not film, this is real
and it's happening to a man
who was once an infant and cried in the dark

Those are real intestines
spilling out into his hand;
the pain and terror are real

Let's begin again
This is a finger
This is an eye

Dear girl, all the women I ever loved
had lovers they wanted to talk about.
Over the years my face
took on the benignity of a priest.

And snow once had the white radiance of a dream,
the air above it sparkling fresh and clean.
I've seen too many sparrows, dead to the world.
If you live long enough, the differences cancel out.

And why do women think their sex life
so fascinating? Or is it disillusion, cold lust,
makes them go on the way they do,
blabbing their silly hearts out?

This life's a cauchemar,
a savage dream from which we never waken.
The roulades of energy are all that matter,
not recollections on a windswept moor.

Ask the malign fates: women adore mass killers
whose members they stiffen to wave
like Mozart's magic flute over the dead,
lying huddled against the cold in fosse and ditch.

His old fingers making wet
the hairy monster under her lace tunic,
he hears the deft-handed goddess
tell across the torn coverlet
how once, still a copper-haired *kori*
in Piraeus,
she watched her grandfather
slit the pig's throat
ear to ear;
afterwards hearing
the hot blood of the crazed animal,
dying on his four trotters,
spurt into the white enamel pot;
all the while thinking
of the small fast thunders
the first gouts of rain
made on her roof,
the wind howling all night long:
a decrepit satyr lost
briar-trapped in a dark, dank grove
and in pain.

He was telling me
how important love was,
lamenting the atrophy
of human emotion
in our mechanical age.

It was apparent
he was well up
in Lawrence and Kierkegaard;
moreover, the man was sincere.

Even if, later,
he deliberately flicked
his cigarette ash
into a flowercup
where a black insect
was crawling.

But neither the sizzle
nor the scream
(which I alone heard)
interrupted his excited
words of love.

RUNTS

After Auschwitz and Gulag
who can be cynical?

Cynicism belongs
to an earlier, more innocent age,
one whose false glaze an idealizing
Christianity and Romanticism
gave birth to and shaped

Nowadays we know
perversities of every kind
horrendous brutality
lies treacheries betrayals
the delights of sadistic impotence
are normal
and nothing to be upset by,
being the ugly and thwarted blooms
of the *Wille zur Macht*

One simply learns
to protect himself against
that most dangerous animal of all, Man;
luckily in this century
thanks to science & civilization
wolves and tigers
are no longer a problem

Runts are the problem,
runts who long for the stride and stature
of giants; who hate all truth-telling mirrors.
History demonstrates
outbreaks of runtishness
occur with rhythmic periodicity,
therefore have a small hydrogen bomb handy
or better yet become an Israeli citizen

Reflect long and hard
on these matters, my children,
though poets, fabulists, theologians, anarchists
and other amiable liars
go on prattling as before

At night even the most luminous stars
mock the red-eyed crone
with their leaden silence

Mere bunion-sore bit of flotsam,
mornings she leaks her migraines
into the naked sea,
promising greater ones to come.
That'll give it something to growl about, she croaks,
and calls the empty noise cosmic drivel.

A leaf settles on her pointed shoe.
God's shedding his dead skin.
Will she catch the ontological drift
of His speech? See Omnipotence in waves' boom?
Majesty in the fall of a leaf?

Once, not too long ago,
on a ravaged plain laned
with the corpses of brave men,
I saw God in full regalia
of flaming mortars and thunderbolts;
howitzers spat out His anger.
That day I had no fear.

That day
God looked straight at me
through the crazed eyes
of a Nazi airman
blubbering to his bleeding stumps.

So expertly did he teach
his Jewish mistress
the art of love-making

that now
when she goes down
on her newest lover
– a much-troubled Austrian

he moans with ecstasy
and babbles
          he no longer
sees his father's polished
boot
      pressing for gold
in the bone-rubble
of Belsen and Dachau

Desire
without reverence

is lust.

I know that
   by the way
my phallus stands up
at sight of you.

I could stab
you
   with it,
plunging it again
   and again
into the vile softness
   of your body
that I might see
your eyes glaze up
with death
   as once with sex.

Once the arms
that held you
   held glory,
held love and delight;
now when I leave
your embrace
   small vipers
fall from my moist armpits,
vermin,
and I am sick with hate.

Their SS collars unbuttoned,
the Austrian officers
ordered the Jewish children
brought into the mess
in groups of seven.

Smiles, affectionate pats
soften the children's faces;
gifts of dolls, toy trains.
Some of the younger officers
are plainly moved.

When the last glimmer of suspicion
fades, the officers whip out
their revolvers
and start shooting.

Then the next batch is called for...
and the next... and the next...

Because he was not made
into a detergent or blue lampshade
proud, proud
he represses a faint smile
– his wreath for those who died.

And because
he watched the vile impalement
of his father, this one
a veined light has in his eyes,
interesting to himself and others.

In the trembling brake
such an odd smile
have serpents in profile;
such a veined light
have their knitted coats.

Lucky stiffs
to have escaped
            unharmed
from the most ferocious beast
in creation

Not to have been gassed
or sizzled
not to have been shot
or your skulls split open
with a crowbar
not to have had molten lead
poured down your throats
but like the good bourgeois
you were
to own your own graves
and lie there moldering
            peaceably
into the earth

Your descendants
will be even luckier
if they're never born

Me? I feel safest in cemeteries.
Horizontal humans lie peacefully;
no anger or mischief in them, no hate
and deceit. Even if darkness comes
when I find myself standing near a slab
time and fierce squalls have tilted towards me
so that I think of the moles underfoot
tearing the flesh clean off the skeletons
I have no fear or sadness. Why should I?
The dead are surely more fortunate
to be done at last with life's ills and chills,
with the lies needed for mere survival
and the mean compromises each must make
before he can call some small space his own.
Bah! The comedy's not worth a frog's fart;
only priests and rabbis think otherwise,
metaphysicians and crazed bolsheviks.
For myself, I love the tranquil boneyards
both for the evergreen moral they teach
and for the asylum they give against
the violent longings that agitate
the caged animals of Chicago
and Madrid, of Moscow, Belfast and London.
Tombs, I say, are reassuring when men
are swine, smiling wolves with capped teeth,
the cities reeking of scribbling whores
and those who need no bribes to pimp for them.
To these, O Zeus, send plagues! Destroy them all!
Don't leave behind a single specimen
and rid earth of locusts, snakes, and weevils;
let the new seedlings come up tall and green.
Preserve all poets mad and marvellous,
guard them from the fury of envious dust.

You made sausages and you survived

The Hitlerites made in Kiev
a desolation,
flinging the corpses
into the deep ravine, Babi Yar;
then came the turn of the Bolsheviks

You escaped both plagues

"The world is big," you explained,
"and a sausage-maker will never be lost."

Poets turn shit into poems
and plaster them on slaughterhouses:
but the smell comes through

Ah, that smell:
it takes blood and plenty of guts
to manufacture it;
also hacked flesh

Wiser than Plato and Christ,
more truthful than any poet who ever lived,
you turned horsemeat into sausages
and sausages into gold

There should be a monument to you
in every big city of the world

For patriotic reasons, or for socialism or nationalism
people curse one another
torture, maim, eviscerate, kill;
and strike down little children, even babies
They do all this
because they are themselves cursed,
they have had an evil spell put on them
and must act out their parts;
the regional costumes and weapons
were long ago selected for them
and the deaths they will accomplish
were long ago willed as their doing
It is they and no one else
who must compose that firing squad
destroy that town or city
sentence that spy to death by garrotting
unreel the fine-meshed net of hate
and hang canisters on every loop
to explode at the lightest touch

We shall come to love by and by
over heaps of burnt corpses
over the mutilated bodies of children
through destroyed homes where only the doorposts remain
We shall come to love
when ashes and rubble heaps are the black divisions
on our compass
but not now, not yet

We have not suffered enough
we have not killed enough
we have not maimed enough
we have not massacred enough old men and women
we have not amputated enough limbs of young men
we have not blinded enough infants in their cradles

There are still regions on our planet
human blood has not made wet
valleys and mountains that have not heard
the sound of human groans and wailings
forests that have never witnessed
human treachery and human vindictiveness
sunsmitten gorges that have not echoed and re-echoed
with the searing cries of hate and triumphant carnage

The Messiah will come
only after every inch of earth has been stained with human
blood
only after every lake, river and sea has been polluted
with the corpses of butchered men and women
only when the air is made thick with the moans of victims
expiring with indignity and extreme pain
only when all nations have tumuli of slaughtered humans
on which he can step as he makes his way to his seat
on the highest mountain

The Messiah will come
when the maimed and mutilated, the weeping and suffering
in all lands, in every valley, mountain, and plain
agnize the universal heritage of evil,
turning curse into blessing,
and redeemed,
embrace joyously their common tie,
their bond and brotherhood
in death, in dying

Strong in cunning
and implacably cruel

Man slays his kind,
kills them without pity or remorse

Yet their numbers increase
till they cover the earth

Miracle, O Lord,
or Shaitan's enduring love and concern?

THE VIOLENT LIFE

For Pier Paolo Pasolini

Your beautiful Marxist head
                                smashed
lies in the dark wood

The chilled red cells
that once held the passion of Christ,
a dream of social justice
                                    indiscriminately wet
dirt road, insensate twigs and grass
the lout's crude wooden bat

Finally
at peace forever with the violent life

Everyone laughed when he told the assembly
how the famous rebel poet was captured.

They laughed even louder
when he described for them
with many jokes and asides
the next day's activity.

How they had pulled his ears
away from the skull
and made him chew and swallow them,
first one then the other.

Because they had seasoned
the bleeding ears with Fr. mustard
his compatriots, when they see him,
laughingly cry to one another:
"There goes Moutarde."

The sight of his earless head
cracks everyone up
even at funerals
and solemn commemorative parades.

Everyone says
he's eligible for a pension.

He drowns his fear of death
in his enemy's life-blood
and with smoking hands
pulls down peace
from the glaring skies

Under a blanket of carnage
that hides him from the terror
tormenting him without cease
he plagues himself
with dreams of sainthood

Soul encased in rotting flesh
god with an asshole
he shapes the humbling stool
into catafalque and bomb,
immortal poem

The word betrays the act;
The act alone is pure.
The rest is literature:
Fishbait for fools and pedants.

Look at that mountain back,
Knife-edge poised against the sky.
A single bird flies over it
And disappears.

At that height nothing dies;
All is unyielding, eternal.
And I imagine the cries
Of the unsacrificed birds.

I image the only music
I hear – soundless, unchangeable.
I am in love with silence,
With the hardness of silence.

I shall become
Like that stone
Through whose single cleft
Flows the stillest water.

A spider danced a cosy jig
Upon a frail trapeze;
And from a far-off clover field
An ant was heard to sneeze.

And kings that day were wise and just,
And stones began to bleed;
A dead man rose to tell a tale,
A bigot changed his creed.

The stableboy forgot his pride,
The queen confessed an itch;
And lo! more wonderful than all,
The poor man blessed the rich.

VENI, VIDI, VINCI

Hear wisdom, my son,
Hear wisdom and live:
Heroes win medals
That smart men give

O . B . E .

How delicately
the Englishwoman
scratches her rectum

Firmly, yet gently,
and with what a regard
for the decencies

Centuries
of imperial rule
inform that touch

Ladies, your unlived faces
innocent and old
are caught up with footfalls
dying in the turquoise air.

Ladies, making a ceremony
over the hot scones and tea,
God hoofless beyond roofs
pipes resevoir music
for your imaginary appetites.

Ladies, why do the refractory
mirrors reject you; and why,
the eccentric stranger
meditating on suicides
and the conception of bats,

Am I suddenly made sad
with an illusion of two heads
framed by coffins,
the coiffed ringlets still moist
going dry on dry
impeccable skins?

A death's head
from which falls away
a black soutane,
he conducts me
and the three withered nuns
from Pamplona
through his catacomb of horrors.

Complete with hairy lip
and decaying stumps of tooth,
the three withered nuns
from Pamplona
kiss relic and bloodstained bars
asking for intercession.

As they kneel and mumble
I hear reverberate
in cave and cell
the running bulls of Pamplona.

Her face and teeth yellow from the christs
she embraces idiotically in her sleep;
her arms long and thin like wax tapers;
her eyes red, their sockets preternaturally deep.

Her lips cracked, from churning prayers;
the spittle – like pus in an infection –
manifesting how the soul has agents
to surround and grapple with each heavy sin.

On her untidy dresser pills by the dozen;
medicaments, loose hairs, syrups "pour la rhume";
encompassing me, a sour body odour
vindicating empirical Hume.

Poor ignorant lass whom evil priests
like incubi from a foetid ditch
have sucked dry and left your very nipples
mis-shaped, and black as the hat of a witch.

The rain falls on the street.
All this day I have passed
Thinking of your deceit:
Betrayals born of lust,
A woman's vanity.

If I rail who hears me?
Hearing, what man won't grunt?
Open a vicious eye
And say the world's a sty;
You – its prized ornament?

Shall I speak of honour?
Among liars and thieves?
He pants to get on her,
Warm nose in her cockmuff
That sneers the slut deceives!

The rain smashes the leaves
And blurs the windowpane.
Let poets say it grieves.
"Money and a good stuff"
I think is its refrain.

A modern man can't curse:
Lust is your best excuse.
Yet shall my speech be coarse;
My angry words a fuse
Smouldering in a verse.

There is no right or wrong,
Love is a madman's dream
And I must hold my tongue
Where pigs and pygmies roam
And you're my queen, my quean.

VILLE MARIE

Thérèse who died of that or this
Hath made a miracle for us:
Her blood now prinks in every arc
And neon crescent after dark.
Her soul, a glass bead, lights the sky.

And like a swarthy Jesuit
Mount Royal grips its burning cross
Where every sacred bulb is lit
By some pure soul who dwells in it.
Sparrows and virgins glorify.

Observe the stricken – bent in prayer –
Like glistening snails upon the stair:
Mute fifty years, the voiceless talk,
Old cripples dance before they walk
The stone-blind see
And only poverty
Finds no cure there.

Hush, the jewelled hour has come
When saints and birds are dumb
– After a famine or a fire
God for a toothpick plucks a spire!

Your words were not meant for *goyim,*
for necrophiles and ill-natured scum:
for the forever damaged humans
sloth and impotency have made vindictive.

Joyous people should have heard your *meshalim,*
only those who glow with an inner fire
and need neither possessions nor fame
to achieve an illusion of abundance.

In century after century
the gentiles have poured your rich blood
into their boredom and futility:
it soothed them between their reeking infamies.

Shlemihl! You should have preached only
to the converted, the happy extravagant few
and left the fierce cripples of the world
to smash their crutches on one another's heads.

MALE CHAUVINIST

God never once asked Mary
whether she wished her womb to be
a vehicle
for the Immaculate Conception

Like any unthinking man
He just blazed away
and let it happen

Poets have easy tears
for what they imagine
is your predicament:
tears but no solutions

And Switzerland exports
like wristwatches and cheese
nice-smelling, intelligent women
to teach you their unhappiness

Demagogues with cold eyes
advance on your crumbling doorstep
to amplify your sighs
into a peal of thunder

Time doubtless has griefs stored up
for you dazed and gross as the earth
and your tiny son that hangs
like a black pendant under your chin

Smoke your hookah forever
and give suck to your baby
O perfect symbol
of stupor and fertility

APOSTATE

Having explored Blake and Lawrence
with me;
having heard me discourse on Nietzsche
and his loathing for the bourgeois
                              for his lackeys and tools;
and listened with both shapely ears
as I railed like monk or madman
at civilization's hypocrisies

You yet handed over
                    to Bay Street lawyers
poems and love letters
I had penned for your eyes only

For this odious apostasy
may your name and Judas self
be forever anathema to poets and lovers
everywhere,
your capped teeth and all your hair
fall out
      and your vagina
sprout a small blue flower
each time you pass a lawyer

It is not men you fear
but the tenderness they make you feel for them

And your resentment is not against men
but against the unfair division of the universe
into pestle and mortar, mountain peaks and valleys

Dark your beautiful eyes and tragic:
they have seen too many fearsome transformations
of smooth pluckable mushrooms into clubs and truncheons

Your desirable breasts are a burden to you
and though your Caesarean cicatrice
is an arrow that points directly
to where all men and angels would wish to lie,
your supple pleasure-promising legs are closed
against them like inhospitable Abrahams

Unsure of the planets that rule, finally
you walk away hand-in-hand with your pride
leaving behind your modern confusion
for philosophers to unravel

Here parasites thrive, niggardly worms, merchants
That grow sleek gnawing on sculpted stone;
Unabashed they traffic in greatness, selling
Lustrous names as if these were patents
Only themselves and their children own:
Their title deed any tourist's map of Florence.

No laughter or music. No noise of revelry.
The bourgeois faces grey-glum as the houses
Shuttered and dark in the lengthening dark nights.
The streets stink of leather, of expensive jewellery
And Europe's discredited culture cattle
Running in a delirium to fondle and buy.

Everywhere the alluring baubles on display
To bait lovers or to bankrupt husbands;
Masterworks of energy and delight
From the ends of elegant neckchains sway
Or memorialize a brand-new pepperoni brand
With only Dante's silent bust to scorn and flay.

Forgive me Cranach, Lippi, Michelangelo
And ring, mournful bells, over their master canvasses;
Tomorrow I'll take an axe to all the famous statues
Of beefed-up pagans, hack them with one blow
And razing the Uffizi and the Pitti Palace
Dump rubble and rabble into the putrid Arno.

Florence,
June 6, 1975

75

They have already consumed the Doges' palace
And it goes without saying the Bridge of Sighs
Misery and a club-footed poet made famous.

Pert and clumsy as the pigeons they feed,
They photograph each other endlessly.
Beer-garden gemüthlichkeit. Also Belmont Park.
The orchestra spiritedly plays the overture
To La Traviata.

Where have I twigged this before?
Ste Agathe? Some other Laurentian resort?
It does not matter.

This is Venice. This is Europe.
And these are Nietzsche's "good Europeans."
Tomorrow they will sprawl on the Lido sand
Getting their legs and torsos tanned.
So greatness is digested. Saint Mark's lions.

Their overtired eyes will close in sleep.
Sleep. Sleep. The sleep of the just cultured.
To eat. To eat palazzos and monuments,
Menu in hand.
"Mesdames e herren, you must eat first
That fine piece of sculpture
And the rest in this order."

While hangs Il Duomo in miniature
From burnt neck or wrist.

Rubbing oils
on herself
she pulls out
a pocket mirror
to take a long look
at a face
that asks
if it is becoming
sufficiently
tanned and sleek
to attract
one of the male flies
buzzing about her breasts
buttocks
and exposed patches
of raw skin
and when he will alight
to inject
the sweet venom
of love
into the receptacle
prepared for it
to round out
the contour
of her belly
with another fly

Book in hand, tree-shade to keep off the sun,
I cried out from my comfortable fence:
"Justice, divine or human, there is none;
   Look at these sweating Spaniards crushing stone,
   Who reeling serve out a lifetime sentence
For a spasm in bed that was not their own!"

They rush into waves that can saw your head off
Or cavort on the beach sand;
Their bodies are angular, athletic,
Adept for war, the sport of love.

Godless sunworshippers, their faith
Is truth, the magnanimity of victors;
Surely they are the proud, self-confident race
The gentle Zarathustra dreamed of.

Like him mistrusting eloquence and rhetoric,
Contemning the poets: camp-followers, liars;
Only from devotion to fact
Will they make a severe and singular beauty.

Having learned finally the world's measure
(A pig's egg contains all its wisdom and justice)
They, rifles and rockets in hand,
Wait open-eyed for the ages to hatch it.

Knowing though evil is the world's primal
Constitution nothing may alter,
The righteous warrior yet has his lonely triumph,
As when clouds part and reveal a star.

PROJECT

See, ah, how stricken, the branches
Of a catalpa drop their shadows
On the ground – a torero's cape.
The sun licks the funeral blobs of shade,
The relentless sun has done the grass dirt.

Near a mound the derelict garden hose
Is coiled cobra-like, digesting the heat.

But the multiple tappings will go on
Till past six. Round me, my hedges,
And this febrile bush some medium
Rears a ghost town of bungalow-duplex.
Clean christians will be here, one synagogue.

There will be a police depot
For vagrant revellers, alien drunks.

I have come face to face with the owners
At evening watering their drives;
I am a most ignorant man,
But is this not new for our days? These wish
Neither to be loved nor written about

And they will endure history
But will neither celebrate nor praise.

So my neighbour, a Greek virgin of fifty,
takes it all out on her poor canine
who's much too dumb to know why she calls him
'she' and washes his underbelly every chance she gets.

Living alone in her many-roomed house,
she troubles my mind, mostly when the dog
barks and barks as if in pain or fearful
of the devil alone knows what. At night

Before I fall to sleep, I hear him whimpering
outside the shut door, bewildered that stroking hands
can roughly seize and fling him on stone steps
and not turn again to fondle, or squeeze his toes.

Each Sunday she greets me on her way to church,
her eyes' happy gleam always making me think
of a sadist who sights for the first time
the white buttocks readied for his stinging rod.

In the afternoon, fat and aproned,
she tends her roses and hyacinths, trims her hedge.
The wornout dog sleeps under the porch.
A light rain washes the roadside dust from the leaves.

A malicious, potbellied, arthritic Jew
sees my head trembling slightly.

A bright hope lights up his eyes
and his smile is one
of pure innocent satisfaction
– it might be Parkinson's disease!

I try to imagine the intense joy
leukemia or a paralyzing stroke
would give him.

When a simple neck exercise
clears up the trouble
the scowl on his face, in turn,
makes me rejoice for days.

In this fashion
do the Chosen People
obey the Mosaic injunction
to make glad their neighbour's heart.

What more can I say? His wife's father's a huckster
who'd sell you two civic statues for the price of one
and throw in a pair of platinum shears
to cut the sky into ribbons.
Her mother goes moodily from room to room
hating herself all day long
but brightening when someone asks her to sing.
The name of Maria Callas brings tears to her eyes.
There's also an importer of Chinese nightingales
from Southeast Asia,
and an old codger who says he can croon
a foetus to sleep. They are all mad in that family
but not dangerous. Mad as ordinary people are,
from boredom, from unfulfilled desires
and from grooming themselves
each morning and watching their vacant faces
grow wrinkles in the round mirror
that stays too expensive to smash.

Friday. Nothing unusual.
   We drop out of the skies
with our picket signs
that read: Free Djilas!

The place: Ottawa.
   The astonished citizens
see us assemble
near the Rideau Canal.

And someone, incredulously:
   What is it?
Who is giving it away?
So I tell him to follow us.

As if sprung from the hot asphalt,
   a line of fierce Ottawans
is marching on the Embassy
for a free Djilas.

He waits in the lawyer's office
till nature compels; then he runs
to ask of the white urinals;
'Has love been distilled into piss?'

Where are the rapt sighings in bed?
The passionate kisses and bites?
The gracious perfumes that fed him
fuel for his exuberant flights?

When he soared above the city
with metaphors and tropes for wings
and wrote into the clear blue sky
'Thrice blessed is the lover who sings.'

More joyous than Shelley's skylark
he was; more arrogant than the hawk,
who now is beseiged by lawyers
and by urinal bubbles mocked

BEUTEL'S NAME IS INSCRIBED
FOR ETERNAL LIFE

As the angry hawk flies towards the sun,
Taking some small creature into the skies,
So shall your fame be taloned fast to mine
And like the clawed rodent rise as I rise.

A native of Kingston, Ont.
– two grandparents Canadian
and still living

His complexion florid
as a maple leaf in late autumn,
for three years he attended
Oxford

Now his accent
makes even Englishmen
wince, and feel
unspeakably colonial.

They all scraped the new shit
off one another's coveralls
and handed the lumps around tenderly
as if they were candied almonds

At the recently completed arsenal
they toasted Lenin's marinated balls
and swore a collective oath before their leaders
to augment the number of flush toilets

Those in shitless clothes they compelled
to undress to the naked skin
but allowed them to choose the excrement
they wished to swallow: pig or human

The slower ones they scourged;
those proud and beautiful were beaten
till the pleased mob heard their skulls crack
and pieces flew in all directions

Then I saw Professors X and Y
wearing identical horn-rimmed glasses
pluck slivers from the red dung
and grinning from ear to ear use them for toothpicks

Hurrah for the elephant
who trampled his trainer to death

Born to captivity
and after thirty years of whipflicks
and love's bullying
saying with his angry hoofs
Take this! Take that! And now this!
for one glorious second he broke free

Hurrah for elephantine dissidence
and death to all Gulag guards and fabricators
Hurrah for life's defiance
of all established routines

Let's erect a monument
to that brave pachyderm
Let the legend of his passover outbreak
be recounted in all the classrooms of the world

ÉLAN

He phoned, the eldest brother,
To ask about his aged mother.
"O she does well," I said,
"Though just now her stern is red
with a large ulcer."
"And doesn't that disturb her?"
"No," I quickly replied,
"It's on the opposite side
to one she had a month ago;
This comforts her so.
She says, 'If ulcers can get around,
So can she,' – and stays above the ground."

BACCHANAL

You there, and you, and you
Come, I want to embrace you
With beer on your breath and halitosis
Come with your Venus-rotted noses

Here is man's true temple, cool
Gloom, sincere worshippers –
Before them the tapers of beer
Like lights lit on many altars

Come, pleasure's my god and yours
Too, to go by your charming noises
Let's hiccup our happiness
And belch our ecstasies to Bacchus

He hears us and sends the room
Spinning. May his touch be always upon us.
May we, as he spins us in the cool gloom,
Be forever in his keeping.

Because last night
my beautiful young neighbour
uncrossed her legs, permitting me
   a glimpse of her white panties,
I can centre my mind on nothing else

Today all afternoon
I've squirmed in my garden
like a pimply faced adolescent
   happy and furtive
under the weakening August sun

No, I do not envy
that composed sunflower
standing proud and upright
   on its long stalk
nor the carefree butterflies

Courting each other
above the innocent cut grass;
nowhere in all nature
   is there anything
like my delicious pain

What does it mean?
Plainly, my dearest friends,
that once again
   I must begin
all over again

CLEAVAGES

A lively Nicoise
fat, fifty, fun-loving, and well-fucked
(Rubens would have delighted to paint her)
starts throwing pebbles
    into the cleavage
of her companion
and soon the two women
their paunchy limbs and faces pink
    from the afternoon sun
are making each other's bosom
    swell bigger and bigger

Not since I was a child
    have I heard such laughter

Seeing them play like this
how can I maintain my hostility
    to the human race,
        keep my gloomy thoughts?

If I had a pink-flushed cleavage
like theirs
I'd join them

STREET VIOLINIST

Someone told him to buy a violin
and pretend he was a musician
down on his luck, he'd get more sympathy
and centimes that way: scrape on the heart
strings and you open the purse. Of course
he plays the same high note over and over,
knowing no other; still, his beggary
is now tricked out in the dignity of art;
and you might say, too, he has become
a sort of street-corner specialist
who gives the one violin note he plays
such a resonance of human distress
no meaner evidence of hardship or defeat
can quite so movingly express

FOR PRISCILLA

Sitting by this idiot
radio
on a windy night
I recall you
tight and impervious
as a pebble
and prototype
of your unmagnanimous sex,
a female hyena
of the spirit
who sniffed the delicious foetor
from my rotting psyche;
and I think whether
the neat dot
of your posterior
incrassating
like a gourd
into the steamy vegetation
of your middle years
will traitorously swallow up
the wedge-shaped virgule
of your back, once,
ah, firm as a ballet-dancer's

I'm not good at giving
the names of bushes;
                    anyway
this was not a bush –
a plant
        that had taken root
away from its fellows
        on the safe ledge;
It was built
                    stubby,
close to the ground
like certain kinds of boxers
            – tenacious –
but it was going somewhere:
            it was on the road.
It did my heart good
            to see it,
like the white leghorn.
                    I watched
crossing the wet field,
            small and arrogant,
his comb a red taunt
            at the vicious weather
– artillerist!

Sitting in a taverna
among garrulous life-loving Greeks,
the morning sunshine
falling on tables and glasses,
I am suddenly pierced
by a Jove-sent arrow
of unreasonable joy

It was Ganymede
who nipped me with it,
a smiling rogue of six
gathering the bottletops
lying on the floor
like fallen miniature crowns
and emptying
their small bowls of sunlight
into his pockets

I greet him
with a secret sign
and my old eyes
are as gay as his

Like
a memory
torn at the shoulders,
my darling
wears
the chemise
I gave her –
a wedding gift.

At night
I tap out
my poems
on her hip bone.

When she can't
sleep
either
we write
the poem
together.

It's when he's drunk
that he knows he should never be married
or have children;
what has he to do
with the conversation of wives
or the chatter and nosepickings of children?
he should be a cloud, a forest fragrance,
a startled fawn, at one
with the elemental force
that makes a plaintain leaf
fall to the ground
or a peacock spread its tail to the sun

I stand on a hill;
my mind reels in terraces
and I'm sucked into a whirlpool
of earth.
An evening wind rattles the almond trees.

In the hushed arena of the sky
the bloodied bull sinks down
with infinite majesty:
the stanchless blood fills the sea.

Triumphant matador, night
flings his black cape across the sky.

THE INVESTITURE

You bend to remove the beachpebble
from your sandal;
and as you straighten to greet me,
your smile, showing your strong white teeth,
reminds me I trod these shores once before.

With a woman who devoured me
as if I were a marine delicacy
snared from its tranquil cove; who,
another Eve, let me discover
evil and creativity are twinned
are one.
        The hills and brackish years between
keep her image in a separate frame.

The same barren hills and widening sea;
the same rumpled many-color'd Joseph's coat,
the same, yet not the same.

For now, my face a warrior's Achaean mask,
it is I who invest these hills, this sea,
with their boundless calm.

Paros,
May 27, 1985

BICYCLE PUMP

The idle gods for laughs gave man his rump;
In sport, so made his kind that when he sighs
In ecstasy between a woman's thighs
He goes up and down, a bicycle pump;
And his beloved once his seed is sown
Swells like a faulty tube on one side blown.

After our love-making
my Greek girl wipes the sweat
from my loins;
then she brings out chilled cucumbers and wine
and setting these before me
commands me to drink and eat.

Why doesn't everyone live
loving and carefree as we do
she wants to know,
a wrinkle appearing
on her forehead
tight as an unripe fig.

When I tell her
not all men are as lucky as I,
she says to lure them
from the battlefields
she would give her small, satisfying body
to all the armies of the world
— even those of Nasser and Hussein
or the despised Algerians.

When I explain laughingly
that the chief attraction
is the chilled cucumbers and wine,
the wrinkle deepens to a frown.
"Ah, that presents a problem," she says;
and my merry Greek wraps me around her,
spilling the white wine.

Though quaint schoolmen
dribble on about myth symbol archetype
and the many masks of W.B. Yeats,
bad one-star movies
are the only cultural indicators
worth attending to

I read off the calibrations
of impotency self-disgust necrophilism,
the meniscus stopping shakily
at that most sinister bar of all:
the swelling hatred between the sexes

In the awful movie
I watched last night
the woman straddles the virginal halfwit,
her arm lovingly around his neck
to urge on his passion

When he comes her pistol goes off
– right in his head

Her mother used to tell her
only bad women
had well-developed busts.

When her young breasts
began to grow
she was certain Herr Satan
had marked her for his own
and would grab her from below.

They grew & grew,
and their very size
has made Gretchen bold:
one fine swing of them, she says,
would knock the devil out cold.

When Eubolus the Greek learned
that his wife had taken
            a lover
he cried a little
            with the smart of it
and then
    to her marvelling delight –
his appetite increased by vanity –
    tupped her eight times
    before the sun roused up:
a phallus hung in the whitening sky
bringing peace to their humid limbs.

LIBIDO

For Joyce Carol Oates

Older, we are on better terms:
no compact signed but the wariness
that comes from experience, the truce
of feudal lords weary after many wars
over nothing.

　　　　　For Nothing is emperor here,
overlooking all, whose ambassador Death
is always on the lookout for lesions,
the thunderclap of a fractured heart.
Meanwhile I line my alive skull with canvases
Id paits for me as artist-in-residence
when he's not screwing the ladies
or making the dummies screech with laughter
in a movie house whose lights dim
moment by moment around faces
blackening suddenly like flashbulbs. Mindless,
in antique costume of criminal or saint
he scours the alleyways for the numinous sadist
who made Spirit his sibling rival,
his checkpoint charlie.

　　　　　O look for him there
in that no-man's land where the fiercest wars
are fought to a sanguinary end
not by nations or classes, male and female,
but by Antagonists whose mottled troops they are
and whose murdering forays will cease
only when this vast sphere is barren and silent
as the scarred slopes that lead on to Aetna.

At home, lying on my back,
Lying with perfect stillness I saw
The scene dispose itself differently
Like a backdrop held by an enormous claw:
On either side the even expensive
Sod; the bungalow with the red border
Of roses; the woman past her middle years
In gaberdine shorts, and her hard fists
That held in place over her suntanned knee
A book, half-shut, in spectacular covers.

And building up the summer afternoon
Music that came thudding upon the air
Music that came it seemed from nowhere
But came in fact from the vacant bedroom
And came from a persistent gramophone tune

Did I contrive this, or did I inerrantly see
The line of hair on her lip?
Surmise her frown? Her talipes?
Did the enchanted hour suddenly darken?
And did the roses
Really uncurl and stretch upon their stems
And order their ignorant centers
Toward the chill anonymous tune,
Then abruptly with the afternoon
Erupt into thick ash against the window frames?

he lives life without fuss
or explanations
    cutting grass, trimming
trees and hedges
    an octogenarian's soundness
in all his motions;
half-French, half-English
of the two solitudes
he's made one large tranquillity
of acceptance
    and has never listened
for the bitter songs
wounded self-love hums
    in the ear
of impotence and defeat
wanting no man's pity or compassion,
least of all
    of poets pandering
to their own weakness
    only
the remaining strength
in his seven good fingers
    disease
hasn't twisted
    into black unfeeling claws
and the bite of a solitary tooth
standing firm
    in his jaw
like a weatherbeaten nail
for his smile to hang on

1 / Since the writings of wise men
    Are my chief study
    I am not like you, Lu Du,
    A close observer of the habits of birds.
    On the other hand I am curious about people.
    I find their inexplicable cruelties
    A matter for sorrow and reflection.
      Nonetheless my lovers say
    The birds chirping in their green coverlets
    Gossip about my merry heart
    And to please me further exclaim
    They make nests from my smiles.
    Why is it I have never once heard
    Such reports about you
    Who have studied the doings of birds all your life?

2 / To eat, drink, fornicate
    And to rail at priests –
    Was it for this
    I was shaped nine months
    In my mother's womb?

3 / When I was young I quarrelled with everyone. I put
    Away my wife because she was fat and would not diet.
    I took up soldiering since killing was agreeable
    And the pay was good. When the victorious general
    Disbanded his troops I found a soft berth
    As his Keeper of Stores where my arrogant manner
    Earned respect from the several factions. Age
      And repeated sickness have at last brought me here.
    I have learned humility and compassion.
    Yet tell me, my sorrowful patient friend,
    When I was acquiring such distinguished virtues
    What were the long graveworms doing? Procreating.

4 / This man loves intrigue.
   I have known him to upset a plan
   Which he himself in great secrecy had set afoot.
   In that way he maintains a good opinion of himself
   And feels himself masterful.

5 / Having seen a drunkard stagger home,
   And a philosopher pitched headlong onto the street
   Because he could not pay the rent,
   And a poet befouling himself in the ditch
   I have shut myself away
      From such disturbing occurrences.
   All the motions of living are equally absurd
   But one might as well have clean linen.

ARAN ISLANDS

Dun Aengus

High walls ... of stones;
man-humbling cliff and shattering sea;
ramparts:
trenches of stone, fierce four of them
and in-between
prehistory's barbed wire, *cheveux de frise*
...of stones.

Enclosing a mist.

Gone are the defenders;
gone, they who attacked.

Nothing here:
only mist
and blue-grey stones.

Cliffs of Moher

At last, as in a dream,
I've come to the cliffs
from where God hurls down
His enemies, every one.

Rat-faced cunning mercers
with a rat's delight;
all, all who are dead of soul,
male and female.

See, their polls open like flowers
on the black rocks below;
their brains dance with the foam
on a green wave's tow.

I sat where Grenadine kings
had once swept by,
thinking on Rey Boabdil
the last and unluckiest of them
– pleasure-loving, melancholy poet
unapt to defend himself –
and my heart went out
to those proud, indolent lovers of beauty
who had taken no cognizance
of death
but out of fountain and fern
had composed a poem
of living, perpetual praise;
and I arose, startling
the scented shadows from their flowerbeds,
and the painted birds from their bough
to cry from my desolate tower:
"I am a Moor
I have come home, I have come home!"

When I look back upon my life.
   What do I find?
   What do I find?
A single star, when I was seven,
That lit up earth and heaven;
   And here and there
   Some few wise and fair
But most, alas, unkind, unkind.

When I look back upon my days,
   What do I see?
   What do I see?
A thrush that sang from a windowsill,
Soul and ears to have their fill;
   But neighbours cried
   And my joy denied
And scared that bird, that bird, from me.

When I look back but yesterday –
   Ah, what befell?
   Ah, what befell?
A woman I told of bird and star,
Gleams and sounds that come from far;
   She brought me here
   Without sigh or tear
And bid me sing, but sing of hell.

Through the loving contemplation
of transiency and mutability
I received a foretaste of eternity
and saw with luminous certitude
that the wheel turned and did not turn

Drawing a roseleaf for ten years
I flowed at last into the leaf;
I shuddered at the raindrop's touch
till I became raindrop and splash:
now I draw the roseleaf perfectly

You are water and like water
slip through the fingers of my hand;
none can hold you, she said gaily,
none can hold you nor will I try.
But she froze me with her cold breath
and where she froze me there I stand.

Good poems should rage like a fire
Burning all things, burning them with a great splendour.

One wrapt flame at noontide blends
The seer's inhuman stare, the seaweed's trance.

And poems that love the truth tell
All things have value being combustible.

Out of rubbish burning and burning comes
Mozartian ecstasy leaping with the flames.

When reading me, I want you to feel
   as if I had ripped your skin off;
Or gouged out your eyes with my fingers;
Or scalped you, and afterwards burnt your hair
   in the staring sockets; having first filled them
with fluid from your son's lighter.
I want you to feel as if I had slammed
   your child's head against a spike;
And cut off your member and stuck it in your
   wife's mouth to smoke like a cigar.

For I do not write to improve your soul;
   or to make you feel better, or more humane;
Nor do I write to give you new emotions;
Or to make you proud to be able to experience them
   or to recognize them in others.
I leave that to the fraternity of lying poets
   – no prophets, but toadies and trained seals!
How much evil there is in the best of them
   as their envy and impotence flower into poems
And their anality into love of man, into virtue:
Especially when they tell you, sensitively,
   what it feels like to be a potato.

I write for the young man, demented,
   who dropped the bomb on Hiroshima;
I write for Nasser and Ben Gurion;
For Krushchev and President Kennedy;
   for the Defence Secretary
voted forty-six billions for the extirpation
   of humans everywhere.
I write for the Polish officers machine-gunned
   in the Katyn forest;
I write for the gassed, burnt, tortured,
   and humiliated everywhere;

I write for Castro and tse-Tung, the only poets
    I ever learned anything from;
I write for Adolph Eichmann, compliant clerk
    to that madman, the human race;
For his devoted wife and loyal son.

Give me words fierce and jagged enough
    to tear your skin like shrapnel;
Hot and searing enough to fuse
    the flesh off your blackened skeleton;
Words with the sound of crunching bones or bursting
eyeballs;
    or a nose being smashed with a gun butt;
Words with the soft plash of intestines
    falling out of your belly;
Or cruel and sad as the thought which tells you "This is the end"
And you feel Time oozing out of your veins
    and yourself becoming one with the weightless dark.

I tell you, William,
there isn't a ghost
of a chance
people will be changed by poems.

Book Club editors
wish to believe otherwise,
Commencement Day orators
and commissars;
but we poets know the facts of the case.
People will remain stupid and deceitful,
their hearts will pump
malice and villainy
into their bloodstream forever.

All the noble lines of poets
did not make Hiroshima and Belsen
not to happen,
nor will they keep back the coming holocaust.

Why should you add
to the mischief,
the self-deception?
Leave that to the culture-peddlers.

Be truthful:
tell children who their forebears were,
the curse they bear.

Do not weaken
even a single one of them
with fine sentiments!

If you or I
should thoughtlessly
commend the verse
of another failed poet
his speech falters
– his cheek goes
red and white by turns.

It is however
this flux and reflux
of colour
      which fans
the small emication
of his talent.

"What would you do
if I suddenly died?"
"Write a poem to you."
"Would you mourn for me?"
"Certainly," I sighed.
"For a long time?"
"That depends."
"On what?"
"On the poem's excellence," I replied.

Harvard and English mist;
the sick Christian;
the American tourist
with an interest in monasteries
rather than castles:
in shrines for aging knees;
a zeal for poetry without zest,
without marrow juices;
at best, a single hair
from the beard of Dostoievsky.

Vain and multivalent as all Jews have been
– half-ass playwright, fop, boulevardier
and Viennese decadent with death in your nostrils –
your poet's vision powered a flight of bullets

Alternately racked by melancholia and fervour
and taking all of Europe for your stage
you peopled it with kings, intriguers, sultans, popes
yourself least aware where truth began, feigning stopped

Self-hypnotized as maddened poets anywhere
charismatic fraud and lovable charlatan,
you dared will fantasy into stubborn political fact
undaunted that all dreams birth the discrepant act

And just when old kingdoms, old philosophies
were dissolving into *fin-de-siècle* crimson mist
and Hegel's conquering World Spirit hovered
on ominous wing over the gutters of Vienna

Your magic raised a nation out of bloodsoaked ruts;
from crowded halls rose the dust whom cossacks
and renowned statesmen and priests had thwacked
into the slums of Europe's festering capitals

Who but yourself, Herzl, ever turned stagecraft
into superb statecraft? Lord Byron, true poet,
tried and failed. D'Annunzio. You only would get
vision and energy into one brilliant, flawless act

So all his passion has shrunk to this:
Three deathless poems and an old hag's kiss.

Repression is here, and so much failure.
And so much suffering. Each one accompanying death
   With mincing steps, with horrible gestures.
And their poems? The pepperminting of bad breath.

The nerved-up lines jerkily
trying to keep pace
with the horror

              to outfox it
perhaps even outrun it
for the Governor General's medal

Whatever the notations of pain:
the crab's severed claw,
the penknife beside the woman's
bleeding cunt,
the putrefying snake

              its sweet stink
in the summer dry grass
...to appear always cool,
never raising the voice
in anger or revulsion
...the perfect drawing-room voice
for Canada's gentility

Life's gross indecencies
of killing & fucking
vised expertly in lines
to fall like icicles
on eyes & tongue

But the sacral odour
is ineffaceable
and finally suffocates

Alas, poor Yorick,
there's vanity even in that;
in going down for the last time,
a soulful look in your eyes
for the photographers

Even the self-disgust
is a kind of pleasure
                    obscene
you keep telling yourself
because you're civilized
and thrill to Mozart & Saint Joan

After a volcano erupts
ornaments and charms are shaped
from the boiling lava
propelled down mountainside and slope.

You can buy them
for a song in Sicily or Yucatan
to wear as a talisman
on bared arm or wrist.

So have I made poems
from the black, scalding dross
that poured out
from my raging breast.
Take whatever you wish or can
but don't overlook those
with a harsh, singular beauty
in their carved nakedness.

The jungle is, and is not, everything.
Culture is, and is not, everything:
but the buttocks
and breasts of the Mexican women
    have something to them; as have
the enormous frogs that made a mess
of our woven carpets, the dogs sniffing,
and the flies everywhere:
(Evil is in the woof of reality
yet the whole is good, is good!)

And when, ah, a young cow submerged,
for a long time
    I wondered what that meant.
The water rippled over the unseen tail
and I thought of eddies, and galaxies,
    and fierce reptilian orgasms.
O time flowing invisibly through wet hairs!
O constellations and death!

Nevertheless, we have arrived
    after looking death in the face
and giving money to beggars
(I give, therefore I am)
and finding, after much travail,
after much meditation
    in deserted village squares,
out of the jungle come the singing birds
and all turns by design
in my mind, O Love.

And the little hills are something
one travels up and down.

Give me, Dark One, these
A woman's white knees
A woman's fine eyes
Her hot, lathered thighs

The nuptial embrace
The first look of love
A bird, sparrow or dove,
The unscheming face

Any bloom, a rose,
Creation's frenzy
The thrill of pity
– The rest is prose.

POLE-VAULTER

Now that grey fluff
covers my chest
and it's the glasses on my nose
that sparkle, not my eyes,
what the horny girls
                want from me
is advice on
how to allure young men;
                      those
with ideas in their head
and pimples on their ass,
my final opinion
on the Theaetetus

They say at my age
I should be guru or sage,
not foolishly behave
like passion's slave

Ignorant trulls
in a cold land;
age will dry their flesh
and wrinkle it with useless folds.
Spry and drugged with love
I pole-vault
           over my grave

ETRUSCAN TOMBS

For Dante Gardini

Being so close to death
so many times
why should you be moved, as I am,
by these offenceless ruins?

I ask pardon for my abstracted gaze,
my impatience with your slow speech,
your gentle all-forgiving smile.
I did not spend my best years
in a concentration camp;
no vile humanoid ever
menaced me with gun and whip
or made me slaver for crusts
urine-soiled and stale;
no officered brute made me kneel in shit.

Here beside you in this remote scene
I feel death's cold finger on my skin,
making it twitch like a fly-stung mare's.
Yet these blank eyes sculpted
from grove and hill and rock
before which the centuries have passed unseen
comfort me; inuring me, I say,
to the sorrows our humanity
compels us to inflict on each other.
They teach me to live the free hours with gusto.

Nothing endures for ever.
Your pain, my pleasure,
the seconds bear away;
our flesh, Dante, one day
will be such golden dust
as a storyless wind stirs
in an empty vault.

Norchia,
Sept. 18, 1984

133

Were Death a woman I should never die.
So jealous is my loving wife that I
Could look upon a passing hearse and sneer
At this dumb show of frail mortality.
For what from Death would I have then to fear

Who might not even by her darkest guile,
Her frowned commands, her most sensual smile,
Tear me from my Love? Tell me, who'd encroach
On her whose fingers stiffen to a file,
Seeing a woman from afar approach?

No, certainly I shall live forever;
For my dear wife will be immortal too
As one whom Death, androgynous lover,
Rages against my jealousy to woo.
Only by dread compact shall we be free
For waiting Death to ravish her and me.

I just can't take it in
that what I'm looking at
    is your cadaver,
recalling your abundant health
and glistening eyes avid for more life,
the strong sensitive fingers
    that probed for tubers
in the frozen Siberian ground.

This late afternoon
it's cold comfort
    to tell myself
you always enjoyed a good laugh
and now may be sleeping off
the genial cups of wine
you shared last night with a friend
solitary as yourself
in London, Ont.,
    pulling a long face
only to give Death back
some of his own gloom.

With so much dignity in your mien
and a touch of your mother's primness,
it's plain you want to go on
treating that boor
as though he were
one more interrogator,
one more Soviet flunky
    eliciting as always
your absolute silence
your tightlipped disdain
for his peasant gaucheness
as you snap, my dauntless Suzanne,
this last chain of illusion
    and break away
finally and forever free.

When I was a ragged child
alive only with cats and dreams
you'd descend, a fairy princess
remote with charabanc and riches.

Settled in our one comfortable chair
you'd send me out
for your burnt almonds.
How you loved them!

And my errand done,
always, graciously, you dropped a dime
into my moist palm
for a Magnet or Gem.

This morning, the Lord of Israel
sent his angel
to fetch you:
one of his burnt almonds.

March 30, 1985
Montreal

I'll say this for you
you're no respecter of persons
and the palace doesn't exist
you can't explode with a laugh

And though you deal
in corruption all the time
you are incorruptible,
being no bribe-taker

And flattery doesn't
work with you either
nor have you ever been awed
by orders and decorations

I know your way
with oligarchs and despots; you
let them posture a short while
and then you say 'Come' and quietly they go

Sir Mortimer
why did you do it?
Both terror and beauty
lie buried in a mass grave.

After Auschwitz and Hiroshima
who believes in funerals any more,
in the dignity
of dying for Cause or Faith?

You were the singular rod
by which we measured our lives,
its meaning and worth;
in your shadow we threw off radiance.

You were the supreme Antagonist,
majestic and severe;
almost we overcame you
with tragedies and religious myths.

By your excesses
you make a mockery of everything;
show us our lives are merely
a rumble of panic and grotesqueness.

One night beside her spouse suddenly
Her heart was ambushed and her naked
Buttocks quivered with death's agony;
Her shoulders twitched, she gave a low cry.
Love's frolic the weak churl thought and shed
Hot seed against her indifferent thigh.

Over the shoulder
of the sun
throw, March wind,
a ragged coat of cloud.

Gather
at the temples, blood,
and fall dropwise
on the frozen ground,
splintering the windows
in their mourning shadows.

Flap your booted feet
on mud and stone
like a fat penguin,
priest.

And shine, officer,
your bright badge
on the cooling corpse.

Like a long, black nail
the morgue's polished
limousine
holds this day together.

Tired of chewing
the flesh
of other animals;
tired of subreption and conceit;
of the child's
bewildered conscience
fretting the sly man;
Tired of holding down
a job; of giving insults,
taking insults;
Of excited fornication,
failing heart valves,
septic kidneys...
This frosty morning,
the coffin wood bursting
into brilliant flowers,
Is he glad
that after all the lecheries,
betrayals, subserviency,
After all the lusts,
false starts, evasions,
he can begin
the unobstructed change
into clean grass,
Done forever
with the insult
of birth,
the long adultery
with illusion?

Père Lachaise is so peaceful
so elegantly laid out
it affords its foreign visitors
the gloomy pleasure of a Racine tragedy

At the tiered ciborium
my girl observes some humorist
has had his initials engraved
on the letter-box urn: C.M.

Before the neighbouring one,
a dark oblong vacancy,
we embrace and kiss fervently
and then embrace and kiss again

Then lighting a cigarette
we each blow a puff of smoke
and watch it fill the narrow void
before it vanishes into the sunlight

Because there's chaos and betrayal
   in every mortal breath,
men yearn for what is genuine
and name the enticement death

No longer to weave through shadows
   by an uncertain light
but to lie in the healing tomb
wrapped in the long shade of night

The hour when I lose life
My friend made ill by grief
At once takes to his bed
With my poor darling Kit;
Laments in her white arms
My cold expired limbs,
And since her naked flesh
Such perfect marble is
Erects betwixt her and him
A towering headstone.

Alas, his mind is grief-crazed
(Interment all its image)
And into her roomy crypt
His rude memorial
With no delay he slips
While kissings ring its knell.
More! Writes on her mound of tit
A friend's flowing tribute
Spurred on by her frequent sighs
And praise of his merit:
Till he too all distracted
Groans and with a shudder dies!

Her lips were round and full
And to his lap she bent;
He saw no car ahead
And when he came he went.

When it came to Santayana's turn he,
His stomach cancer-riddled, turning sod
Upon the Sisters' white linen, canvassed God,
The Essences and Immortality,

Unriddling to the last. Brave philosopher,
As you piped your wisdom to friends your breath
Doubtless was heavy with puke, taint of death.
But I mean you no discourtesy, Sir.

Socrates did no better with a jest
About a cock; though artful Plato
And seminars've made that damned bird crow
For every longhead pegging out. My guest,

The world's, fare well in Limbo. You dead,
I shall want that bright eye, that huge bald head.

An animal dies
and rots back into the earth

Vanquished crustaceans
are washed up by the tide

A swordfish is hooked
and turned into feces and gas

But a pope greets Monsignor Death
with a mitre on his head

Red slippers on his feet
And formaldehyde in his veins

Death washes the face of the world
like the light-filled water
purling gently over the beachstones at my feet

Eternally and quietly
without cease it does its appointed work
cleansing the face of the world
so that the holy light of joy
may shine in pebbles, sunlit leaves,
flowers and vegetation
and beyond all these, beyond everything,
in the glad eyes of women and men

Molivos,
July 5, 1977

In August, white butterflies
Engage twig and rock;
Love-sheaths bloom in convenient fissures
On a dessicated stalk;
The generation of Time brings
Rind, shell, delicate wings.

And mourners. Amidst this
Summer's babble of small noises
They weep, or interject
Their resentful human voices;
At timely intervals
I am aware of funerals.

And these iambic stones
Honouring who-knows-what bones
Seem in the amber sunlight
Patient and confounded,
Like men enduring an epoch
Or one bemused by proofs of God.

Under the despoiled tree,
her park seat
soft with golden leaves,
the wrinkled
disconsolate woman
crimsons her lips.

A breeze
detaches the last
red leaf
and lays it
at her feet.

Between the fall of one leaf and another
I'm not the same man I was
nor, dear Heraclitus, does one enter
the same woman twice though her love keeps.
Count my days brief or long
they've known beginnings and other starts,
ills, chills and illuminations:
to myself I often seem a flatworm
on a wet pavement before
I change back into the sparrow
that plucks me from the sheltering crack
and flies off with me to the nearest twig.
To eat or be eaten, an illumination
either way. Bacterial light and blight
we serve the Atman
who spends and conserves himself
in the fire and eternal dust
he's made the cosmos run on.
My chills help to warm the sun,
the night wind scores its nocturnes
with my laments. Even from the Führer's ash
good savons can be made
though they'll rub no one's guilts away.
And here's the rub, the moral fly
in the universal balm
that salves our human cuts and wounds.
So be valorous men, dear sons,
yourselves imperturbably
and foursquare to the uprights
bona fide, cartes sur table
with tenacity and vision
and just enough saving compassion
to stay human whatever ills rain down
before falls the next leaf or imperium
ordered to endure a thousand years.

LAKE SELBY

Definitely it's not polluted
since no germ would wish
to be found dead in it,
and also it's absolutely
safe for you and the kids
for however far you walk
into its lukewarm wetness
wavelets sedulously suck-suck
at your hips and navel: believe me
it's hardly worth trying
to drown in it; you'd only
be found sitting on your bottom
and the lake's, rope around
your neck or ankle,
stone heavy in your lap.

My son who is six flatly
refuses to swim in it
though wind and water
drive him crazy with joy,
especially water;
he calls the stuff squishing
through his toes 'sea food'
and wants none of its sliminess;
as he describes it
it's so many vile fingers
clutching clammily at his heels
he has to kick furiously
before they will release him
sputtering with rage
and spitting out mouthfuls
of tepid lakewater and weeds.

Yet the townsmen summering it
in stolid painted cottages

that each year tighten
around the lake like a noose
plunge into the shallow water
with cries of delight and gusto
ha-ha-ing to one another
and trying a hundred-and-one tricks
to amuse the less venturesome on shore;
for hours and hours I watch them
pretend they're bouncing porpoises
leviathans and comical octopi
or cruel-mouthed sharks
to make their beached wives and progeny
wave admiringly and praise;
afterwards, scrubbed clean of grime
and slime, smoking their pipes
they will sit and stare at the lake
which moon and silence have changed
into a silvered apparition
of some lost and perfect island
rising slowly to enchant them
between the dark elms and pines.

INNOCENCE

How does one tell
one's fourteen-year-old daughter
that the beautiful
are the most vulnerable
and that a rage
tears at the souls
of humans
to corrupt innocence
and to smash butterflies
to see their wings
flutter in the sun
pulling weeds and flowers
from the soil:
and that all, all
go under the earth
to make room for more
weeds and flowers
– some more beautiful than others?

In the sun
The chokecherries are a deep red.
They are like clusters of red jewels.

They are like small rubies
for a young queen who is small and graceful.
When the leaves turn, I see her white shoulder.

They are too regal to eat
and reduce to moist yellow pits.
I will let the air masticate them

And the bold maggot-making sun.
So I shall hardly notice
How perfection of form is overthrown.

ARACHNID

Sun-purpled, the clover
bussing the outermost strand
was pure camouflage, as were
the innumerable grasses,
dogrose, timothy, vetch.

Nature's geometry, the exact design.
With what grace so ominous
a contraption held the beauty
of the dying day, the fly
dying with faint and futile buzz.

At 4 A.M.
the mind washes its dirty linen.
Hopeless. It will never get it clean.
Till the late hour counsels resignation.

Unless one's gifted
with indignation and laughter
life's one long accumulation
of griefs and guilts,
stains put there by body and spirit.

Have you known old men
muttering to themselves, hawking and spitting?
That's the soul's sour phlegm they're tasting,
sometimes wiping it on their sleeve
sometimes giving it to the wind.

Old men,
they alone have my charity
mumbling hapless and broken
in the toils of their memories.

Because the glowing morning
Dropped from the rooster's beak
The frozen famous statue
Was too amazed to speak

But watched my mother go and come
Like a fish in an aquarium
Sinister alone
And me upon my boycart throne.

Her cheeks were red with bargains
And she moved to the money cries
Like an enchanted dancer
With wide enchanted eyes.

The yells, the cries were frenzying;
Her cheeks grew pale with bargains:
I laid my boyhood head
Among the golden onions.

Already the sun burns less intensely;
its deepest passion is for other skies, other lands;
wedged between two clouds
it seems embarrassed by its sudden loss of power.
The foam now whitens my melancholy
and even the waves speak in a voice not heard before:
more tumultuous yet sadder
like people who shout at each other
at the end of a love affair.

It makes me think
of quiet Mediterranean cemeteries I've known
to see the sunlight limp across the beach
stuffing black leaves of shadow between the stones:
of old women with white skins
and fields of despoiled windflowers.
Where's its force, its fiery heat?
Is this the July monarch that reigned here? This slave
to a calendar, this enfeebled lecher
with not one good squint, one amorous gleam
left in its red eyes?
Slowly the sun mounts the stone steps of the Plage
and stares at my bronzed chest and arms
like a woman failing to recognize
her former lover.

I shall wander all night and not see
    as much happiness as this infant gives
to his plain sisters who are adoring him
and his mother cradling and covering
    him with her love.

She has borrowed the white moon from the sky
    to pillow his golden curls
and at her magical cry the dark roofs
the length of the street lie down
    like quiet animals.

The night will wear out and disappear
    like soiled water through the city's drains
but now it is full of noise and blessed neighbours
and all the tenement windows fly open
    like birds.

Index of Titles

Index of First Lines